The Client's Guide to Cognitive-Behavioral Therapy

The Client's Guide to Cognitive-Behavioral Therapy

How to Live a Healthy, Happy Life...No Matter What!

Aldo R. Pucci, MA, DCBT
President
National Association of Cognitive-Behavioral Therapists

iUniverse, Inc.
New York Lincoln Shanghai

The Client's Guide to Cognitive-Behavioral Therapy
How to Live a Healthy, Happy Life...No Matter What!

iUniverse books may be ordered through booksellers or by contacting:

iUniverse
2021 Pine Lake Road, Suite 100
Lincoln, NE 68512
www.iuniverse.com
1-800-Authors (1-800-288-4677)

This publication is designed to provide accurate and authoritative information in regard to the subject matter covered. It is sold with the understanding that the publisher is not engaged in rendering legal, accounting, or other professional service. If legal advice or other expert assistance is required, the services of a competent professional person should be sought.

From a Declaration of Principles jointly adopted by a Committee of the American Bar Association and a Committee of Publishers

ISBN-13: 978-0-595-38076-3 (pbk)
ISBN-13: 978-0-595-82446-5 (ebk)
ISBN-10: 0-595-38076-X (pbk)
ISBN-10: 0-595-82446-3 (ebk)

Printed in the United States of America

This book is dedicated to **Maxie C. Maultsby, Jr., M.D.** Dr. Maultsby is an internationally acclaimed psychiatrist and the originator of Rational Behavior Therapy. He also is an advisor to the National Association of Cognitive-Behavioral Therapists.

In graduate school, my focus was on *behavior therapy*, which has very little to do with the important role of thinking in relation to how we feel and what we do. As a graduate student, I bought Dr. Maultsby's book, *Rational Behavior Therapy*, thinking it was a book on how to perform behavior therapy *rationally*. As I began reading the book, I was surprised to discover that Dr. Maultsby's therapy actually was *cognitive-behavioral*, meaning that he helped people by showing them how to change their problem thinking to good, rational thinking. Additionally, although I had been exposed to many different forms of psychotherapy while receiving an excellent graduate education, Dr. Maultsby's therapy was the only one that was based on how the brain works. His book helped me realize that Rational Behavior Therapy was an ideal form of psychotherapy for most people. Therefore, I credit Dr. Maultsby with my becoming a cognitive-behavioral therapist.

As a graduate student, I sent Dr. Maultsby (who at the time was a professor at the University of Kentucky) a handwritten letter expressing to him my excitement over his work. He took the time to reply to my letter and invited me to attend a graduate course on Rational Behavior Therapy that he was conducting in a nearby town. The fact that he even replied to a graduate student's letter was very impressive and encouraging to me. Dr. Maultsby has made many contributions to the field and is world-famous. However, I believe his greatest contribution has been his willingness to be accessible. Although he is a brilliant man, he is very "down to earth." He is an excellent role model for cognitive-behavioral therapists. He presents himself as a Fallible Human Being, just like everyone else. Dr. Maultsby's willingness to respond to a graduate student's letter led that graduate student (me) to years later establish the National Association of Cognitive-Behavioral Therapists.

I know that many professionals, including prominent professors, find it very easy to think of themselves as "above" dealing with anyone who is not on their level professionally. However, any field that wants to grow and improve needs professionals like Dr. Maultsby—brilliant and accessible.

Contents

Pre-Therapy Assessment

Please complete the following questionnaire honestly. This will help you and your therapist assess what you are experiencing, how you are thinking, and how you are feeling.

Circle the answer that best represents your situation.

	Strongly Disagree	Disagree	Neutral	Agree	Strongly Agree
1. Things in my life are different than they should be.	1	2	(3)	4	5
2. People make me upset.	1	2	(3)	4	5
3. I can't stand certain things in my life.	1	2	3	(4)	5
4. I need to think well of myself before I can do certain things.	1	2	3	(4)	5
5. There are things in my life that are simply awful and terrible.	1	2	(3)	4	5
6. How I feel depends on how people treat me.	1	2	3	(4)	5
7. Certain situations make me upset.	1	2	3	(4)	5
8. People can't feel and act better until their situation changes.	1	2	3	(4)	5
9. You can't trust someone again after they have violated your trust.	1	2	3	(4)	5
10. People need to be concerned about other peoples' opinions.	1	2	3	(4)	5
11. I have a right to be upset.	1	2	3	(4)	5
12. There isn't much hope for me to feel or act differently because I have tried before and failed. That means I can't.	1	(2)	3	4	5
13. It's important for me to focus on how I feel and what I do as the main indicators of how well I am doing in therapy.	1	2	3	(4)	5

Pre-Therapy Assessment

Please complete the following questionnaire honestly. This will help you and your therapist assess what you are experiencing, how you are thinking, and how you are feeling.

Circle the answer that best represents your situation.

	Strongly Disagree	Disagree	Neutral	Agree	Strongly Agree
14. If I don't see it, it doesn't exist.	1	(2)	3	4	5
15. I just can't cope with things.	1	2	3	(4)	5
16. I need medication to make me feel better.	1	(2)	3	4	5
17. I believe that if I just get things off of my chest, I will feel much better.	1	2	3	(4)	5
18. If I do something good, I should be rewarded.	1	2	3	(4)	5
19. If I treat people well, they should treat me well, too.	1	2	3	(4)	5
20. If I am the only one thinking a certain way, then I must be wrong.	1	(2)	3	4	5
21. If it feels wrong, it must be wrong.	1	2	(3)	4	5
22. If it feels right, it must be right.	1	2	(3)	4	5
23. It's important for a person to follow his or her gut instinct.	1	(2)	3	4	5
24. If I do something wrong, I should punish myself for it.	1	2	3	(4)	5

Introduction

This book is based on the philosophy and techniques of **Rational Living Therapy**, an approach to counseling and psychotherapy that I have been developing since 1990. Rational Living Therapy is a type of Cognitive-Behavioral Therapy (CBT). The word "cognitive" means "thinking." Therefore, cognitive-behavioral therapy focuses on how people think and helps them to think in ways that makes them feel the way they want to feel and helps them to achieve their goals.

Rational Living Therapy is a very systematic approach to therapy, which means that there is a certain process that the therapist follows, and there is an objective or "point" to every session. This is a book about rational self-counseling. Since you are in therapy, you might be saying to yourself, "I don't want to counsel *myself*, I want my *therapist* to counsel me!" That certainly is an understandable reaction! Keep in mind, though, that all counseling is self-counseling, and the therapist just guides the client through it.

Believe it or not, we counsel ourselves every waking minute of every day. Sometimes we counsel ourselves in a productive, rational manner, while at other times we unintentionally counsel ourselves in an unproductive, irrational manner. Rational self-counseling is something you already know how to do. You could not make it through a single day without some amount of good, rational self-talk. The problem, though, is that we often do not pay much attention to our self-talk, and good, appropriate reactions seem much more like accidents than intentional behaviors.

What most people do not know is how to consistently, intentionally counsel themselves rationally. Why don't they? Because people are not taught rational self-counseling during the normal course of their growing up!

Therefore, your therapist will teach you how to help yourself feel the way you want to feel and how to achieve your goals by teaching you, and showing you how to apply, rational self-counseling skills. These skills will enable you to feel and act the way you want to feel and act, *on purpose*! These counseling skills give people a great deal of confidence that they can make themselves feel good anytime, in any situation.

The Client's Guide to Cognitive-Behavioral Therapy is a comprehensive book designed to enhance your learning of rational self-counseling concepts and techniques. Besides original techniques I have developed, this book is based on the work of pioneers of cognitive-behavioral therapy, including Maxie C. Maultsby, Jr., M.D., Albert Ellis, Ph.D., and Aaron Beck, M.D.

I'm assuming that your psychotherapist, in encouraging you to read this book, plans to help you approach your concerns by using cognitive-behavioral psychotherapy techniques. You will find the cognitive-behavioral approach to be very straightforward, practical, and easy to understand. This manual will help reinforce the concepts and techniques taught to you by your therapist.

How to Read This Book

Self-help books are not designed to be read in the same manner one would read a novel. Novels are read from beginning to end, and once you know the outcome, there is little reason to read the novel again. Novels are designed to be entertaining, not educational. Self-help books, on the other hand, have no plot or storyline to follow. Their purpose is to educate, not entertain (although good self-help books try to present the material in an entertaining way). Self-help books are most effective when they are read at least twice, as most people report a better understanding of the material the second time through.

This book is most effective when each chapter is read several times before moving on to the next chapter. Your therapist will assign chapters for you to read. I recommend that you:

–Spend one week on each chapter;

–After you have read the chapter, read it at least once more;
–Make a note of anything with which you disagree, if that is the case;
–If something doesn't make sense to you, write it down;
–Think of how the topics covered apply to you.

Feeling better takes effort. There is no way to get around that fact. As Dr. Maultsby says, "About the only thing that comes easily to us is trouble." Rational self-counseling is not hard, but it does take practice to apply the techniques to your concerns effectively. It is worth the effort!

What to Expect From Cognitive-Behavioral Psychotherapy

After a good initial assessment (which might last 1–2 sessions), your therapist will begin teaching you rational self-counseling concepts and techniques and will show you how to apply them to your concerns. Cognitive-behavioral psychotherapy is very instructive, so your therapist will spend most of the first few therapeutic sessions teaching you. For people who want to "get things off their chest" the instructional nature of therapy might seem a little disconcerting. However, the instructive approach helps insure that you will feel the way you want to feel and achieve your goals as quickly and as effectively as possible. While teaching you rational self-counseling skills, your therapist will assist you in applying the techniques to your concerns. The beauty of cognitive-behavioral therapy is that while teaching you skills to effectively deal with your current problems and concerns, your therapist will also teach you how to apply those same skills to anything else that might come your way for the rest of your life.

A Simple, But Important Biological Fact
(And Why New Year's Resolutions are Rarely Kept)

Did you know that you, in effect, have two brains? Your brain is divided into two hemispheres—the left-hemisphere and the right-hemisphere, and these hemispheres are connected by a bundle of nerves called the corpus callosum. The corpus callosum allows the hemispheres of the brain to communicate with each other.

When it comes to our emotions, each hemisphere is responsible for different functions. For most people, the left hemisphere is responsible for processing language. In other words, it understands and processes the words we use, hear, and read. The right hemisphere is responsible for producing images. When we imagine, dream, or daydream we are using our right brain.

Our left-brain words trigger our right-brain images, and we tend to act on those images (Maultsby, 1984). When someone says, "imagine an apple," the left brain understands the word "apple" and sends a message to the right brain where an image of an apple is produced.

While the left brain understands and processes every word we use, the right brain understands every word but one—the word "not." Because of that fact, we cannot imagine ourselves "not doing something." We can only imagine ourselves *doing* something.

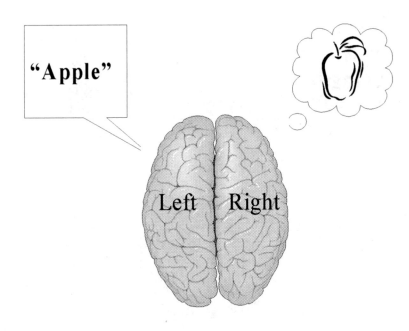

Left-Brain Words Trigger Right-Brain Images

As an example, do this experiment. Please imagine yourself *not* reading this book right now. Were you successful? If you think you were, I'll bet that you imagined yourself doing something else, like watching television or working. Notice, though, that I did not ask you to imagine yourself doing something else. I asked you to imagine yourself *not* reading this book. You cannot do it because our brains cannot imagine *not* doing something. We can only imagine ourselves doing something.

However, many goals are stated in negative terms. Many people, for example, make the resolution, "This year, I am not going to smoke." Have you noticed, though, that most often, when a person repeats such a statement to himself, he ends up smoking anyway? At that point the person usually views himself as "weak-willed" or "too addicted."

While motivation to stop smoking is very important, the manner by which the goal is stated makes a big difference as well. What happens with this behavioral intention, "This year I'm not going to smoke," is that the left-brain understands the sentence, but as the sentence travels to the right-brain, the word "not" is dropped, leaving the sentence:

"This year, I am going to smoke."

The statement, "I'm not going to smoke" becomes,
"I'm going to smoke" when it enters the right brain.
We tend to act on our right-brain images.

The person then unintentionally imagines himself smoking, and acts on that image.

A better behavioral intention would be, "This year, I refuse to smoke, and instead of smoking, I am going to exercise, eat well and chew gum anytime I get the urge to smoke until I have no more urges." A person can imagine himself doing that, and then can act on those images.

Imagine that as you are walking across a tightrope doing your best to get across to the other side, someone yells up to you, "Hey, don't fall!" What would be the very first thing that you would imagine yourself doing? Falling, of course! Instead, if someone were to yell up to you, "Be careful, watch each step," you would be much more inclined to imagine yourself doing just that.

Therefore, when asking yourself or someone else to do something, phrase the request in positive terms. Rather than saying, "Don't forget your homework," say, "Remember your homework." Rather than saying, "I'm not going to yell if my husband yells at me," tell yourself, "I will remain calm and rationally discuss the issue with my husband."

Phrase all of your goals in positive terms—in terms that you can visualize.

Your Goals

Please note that your therapist has no intention of telling you how to live your life or what your goals "should" be. Rational Living Therapists (as do all good cognitive-behavioral therapists) want to know what *you* want out of life. Your therapist then will help you to think and behave in ways that will help you achieve those goals.

Your goals are very important because they give you the reasons to work at feeling and getting better. For example, why would a person be concerned about feeling depressed? Because feeling depressed often interferes with achieving a goal, even if it is just enjoying an activity.

The next few pages provide you an opportunity to write down what your goals are for therapy, what you want on a daily basis, and what you want out of life.

A Very Special Note About Your Goals

When writing down what your goals are for therapy and life,

Refuse to Produce a Filtered List!

What I mean by this is that clients often will only write down what they think is *possible*, rather than writing down everything that they *want*. Therefore, I'm suggesting to you that you write down *everything* that you want, no matter how impossible some things might appear to obtain or accomplish. It doesn't matter if you want a castle overlooking the ocean, write it down! It doesn't matter if you are eighty-years-old and want to be an astronaut, write it down! Write down what you *really* want, not just what you think is possible. Your therapist then will review your list with you and help you to determine, based on the facts, what is possible and what is not. Of those goals that *appear* not to be possible, your therapist will refuse to jump to the conclusion that because the goal seems impossible that it must be so. The more important the goal is to you, the more that you and your therapist will research the topic to see if it might be possible to achieve after all.

If you have difficulty determining "life" goals, ask yourself, "Was there ever a time in my life when I wanted my life to be different than it is right now? If so, how did I want it to be?" Also ask yourself, "When I was a child and an adult asked me what I wanted to be when I grew up, how did I answer that question?"

Often, clients are very happy to discover that what they thought was not possible actually is, or that what they thought would be very difficult to achieve is not as difficult as they had thought. Sometimes, though, clients discover that achieving their goal will take more effort than what they had thought, but that is good information to have. If you want it, go for it!

Also please keep in mind that what you are compiling when you write down your goals and desires is a "wish list" *not* a "have to" list or a "the only way I could be happy" list. This is an important fact to keep in mind because if you happen not to achieve a goal, your brain will allow you to be happy with something else. That is why I subtitled this book, "How to Live a Healthy, Happy Life—*No Matter What!*" There are many roads to happiness!

My Goals for Therapy
(Example)

1. **Do this *more***

– *Ask girls out on dates comfortably*

– *Say "no" when I mean "no"*

– *Hand in assignments on time*

– *Compliment people when they do well*

– *Go to grocery stores comfortably*

Do this *less* (or not at all)

– *Bite my nails*

– *Yell* / Swear

– *Over-eat*

– *Procrastinate*

2. **Emotionally Feel this *more***
(Remember, feelings are one-word adjectives, like happy, sad, excited, anxious, etc...)

– *Happy*

– *Excited*

– *Calm*

Emotionally Feel this *less* (or not at all)

– *Depressed*

– *Angry*

– *Nervous*

3. **Physically Feel This *More***

– *Energetic*

Physically Feel This *Less* (or not at all)

– *Pain in my knee*

– *Headaches*

4. <u>**Think this** *more*</u>

– *That I am somebody*

– *That I can achieve my goals*

– *That girls will like me once they get to know me*

– *That just because things don't go my way doesn't mean I have to be angry about it.*

– *That people do not think bad things about me when they see me*

<u>**Think this** *less*</u> (or not at all)

– *That I'm a nothing and a nobody*

– *That I'll never amount to much*

– *That I'm ugly and everyone who sees me thinks that, too*

– *That it's the end of the world when things don't go my way*

– *That I'll never have what I want out of life*

5. <u>**Know this** *more*</u>

– *How to fix cars*

– *How to figure out what career I want to pursue*

– *How to ask girls out comfortably*

– *How to stop feeling angry*

<u>**Know this** *less*</u> (or not at all)

– *What other people are saying or thinking about me*

My Goals for Therapy

1. **Do this *more***

    Do this *less* (or not at all)

2. **Emotionally Feel this *more***
(Remember, feelings are one-word
adjectives, like happy, sad, excited,
anxious, etc...)

    Emotionally Feel this *less* (or not at all)

3. **Physically Feel This *More***

    Physically Feel This *Less* (or not at all)

4. **Think this** *more*

Think this *less* (or not at all)

5. **Know this** *more*

Know this *less* (or not at all)

<u>Life Goals</u> (Example)

On this page, write down what you want out of life—your long-term goals. In other words, how will your life be when you take a look around and you say, "I like my life because (1) I like where I live, (2) I like who I'm with, (3) I like how I generate income and how much money I have, and (4) I like how I spend my leisure time."

Remember to refuse to only write down what you think is possible. Go for it, and write what you really, really want!

<u>What I want from life</u>	<u>Importance to Me</u> Slightly / Moderately / Very Important
Live near the beach in Florida	*Very Important*
To be able to go to the beach every day	*Moderately Important*
To have a wife and a couple of children	*Very Important*
To have a nice house with a big yard	*Very Important*
To work as a lawyer.	*Very Important*
To retire when I'm 50 y.o.	*Moderately Important*
To earn $100,000 a year	*Moderately Important*
To do things with my family, like going on vacation, sporting events, etc...	*Moderately Important*

To what age do you want to live? _____80_____

Life Goals

On this page, write down what you want out of life—your long-term goals. In other words, how will your life be when you take a look around and you say, "I like my life because (1) I like where I live, (2) I like who I'm with, (3) I like how I generate income and how much money I have, and (4) I like how I spend my leisure time."

Remember to refuse to only write down what you think is possible. Go for it, and write what you really, really want!

What I want from life

Importance to Me
Slightly / Moderately / Very Important

To what age do you want to live? _____

What I Want to Experience and Avoid
(Example)

On this page, write down what you want to experience as much as possible and avoid as much as possible. Spend some time with this and give it some thought as you can use this as a guide for having happy days. Write down everything that comes to mind.

What I want to experience as much as possible

Time with my wife
Time with my children
Football games / Sporting Events
Fishing
My favorite pasta dish
My favorite tv show
Laughing at a funny joke
Reading a good book
A good cup of coffee

What I want to avoid as much as possible

Sinus Headaches
Work days longer than 8 hours
Traffic Jams
Tornados
Hurricanes
Icy Roads
Traffic Accidents
Conflict
Reality TV Shows
Colds / Flu
Being Yelled At
Cleaning Litter Boxes

What I Want to Experience and Avoid

On this page, write down what you want to experience as much as possible and avoid as much as possible. Spend some time with this and give it some thought as you can use this as a guide for having happy days. Write down everything that comes to mind.

What I want to experience as much as possible

What I want to avoid as much as possible

Feelings and Behavior Pattern Form (Example)

Instructions: If you feel or behave in a way that either you do not want or believe might be a problem for you, first, write down in the first column what was going on at the time, what happened, what you were doing, or what you were thinking about. Second, write down in the second column what was going through your mind about what was going on, and third, write down how you felt and what you did.

What happened / What was going on / What I was doing / What I was thinking About	What went through my mind about it	How I Felt / What I Did
My boss told me that I'm fired.	"How could he do that to me? I've worked here for twenty years! He shouldn't do this! I'll never be able to support my family."	Angry & Depressed Went home and went to bed.
My wife told me that I'd better look for a job, or she's leaving me.	"How could she say that? I can't stand that she's putting this kind of pressure on me!"	Angry and Anxious Yelled at her

Feelings and Behavior Pattern Form

Instructions: If you feel or behave in a way that either you do not want or believe might be a problem for you, <u>first</u>, write down in the first column what was going on at the time, what happened, what you were doing, or what you were thinking about. <u>Second</u>, write down in the second column what was going through your mind about what was going on, and <u>third</u>, write down how you felt and what you did.

<u>What happened / What was going on / What I was doing / What I was thinking About</u>	<u>What went through my mind about it</u>	<u>How I Felt / What I Did</u>

1

Let's Get to It:
Feeling Better, Almost Immediately!

Science has yet to improve on Mother Nature at her best—The Human Brain. This is a point that Maxie C. Maultsby, Jr., M.D. (1984) has stressed throughout his career. The brain is capable of triggering very painful emotional reactions. Conversely, the brain is also capable of triggering very pleasant emotions. Since the brain is the organ that controls our emotions, it makes sense to learn how to use our brain in a way that makes us feel good.

Practice the following proven stress-reducing, mood-enhancing techniques daily, and you will very likely begin noticing an improvement in your emotional state.

The Universally Calming Perspective

Dr. Maultsby (1984) developed the following poem to help keep you focused on rational acceptance of undesirable situations:

Even though this is not what I wanted to see....
Until I make it more the way I want it to be....
I shall keep myself pleasantly calm, naturally....
With a warm, soft smile on my face....
I continue to breathe in this slow, relaxing pace....
Until I'm pleasantly calm, naturally....
As I now think it is best to be....

I recommend that you memorize this poem so that you can carry it with you wherever you go; thus, you will be able to obtain almost instant relief in any situation by using it.

Why the "warm-soft smile?" Research experiments have shown that facial expressions trigger chemicals in the brain that produce emotional states. Frowning encourages sadness. Smiling encourages happiness, even if it seems as though there is nothing about which to be happy. Although you might not *feel* like smiling, you probably could at least *squeeze* a "Mona Lisa" smile on your face. Doing so will make a positive emotional difference.

Rational Progressive Relaxation

My tape, "Rational Progressive Relaxation," is a great way to learn to relax quickly and deeply. I recommend that you either purchase this tape (by calling 1-800-853-1135) or have your therapist teach you progressive relaxation as a very effective method of relaxing.

Your Physical Health: Take Care of It!

Your emotions are the result of chemical and electrical processes occurring in your body, and these chemical and electrical processes are affected by many factors. You will learn in the following chapters that you, in effect, direct your brain to produce the chemical changes that result in how you feel and what you do.

Taking care of your body helps you to have a "sound mind." The following is a list of vitamins, herbs, and physical techniques that can assist your body in helping you feel good emotionally. *However, I strongly urge you to talk with your medical doctor about these supplements before taking them, especially if you already are taking psychiatric or other medications.*

Vitamins and Herbs

As you will see in the following chapters, the healthy, un-drugged brain has all the chemicals it needs to make you feel and act better. Therefore, although physicians often prescribe them, psychiatric medications are often not necessary. This is *not* to say that psychiatric medications are not helpful at times, particularly when a person has difficulty benefiting from therapy due to fatigue or concentration problems, or he or she has a problem like schizophrenia or bipolar disorder.

While the following vitamins and herbs are usually not necessary either, it does make sense for us to do what we can to help keep the brain and body healthy so that we are in the best possible position to use them to counsel ourselves effectively.

Research has proven that the following vitamins, herbs, amino acids, and other supplements are as effective as (and sometimes more effective than) their pharmaceutical counterparts, without the negative side-effects usually associated with prescription drugs. These supplements can be obtained at your local health food store.

The "B" Vitamins: Essential for Proper Nerve Functioning

The "B" Vitamins (including B_1, B_2, B_3, B_5, B_6, B_{12}, and folic acid) are essential for proper nerve functioning. "B" Vitamins also play a role in a metabolism. However, emotional distress tends to deplete the body of the "B" vitamins, which sometimes leads to nervousness and decreased appetite. Therefore, most holistic health physicians recommend "B" vitamin supplementation (usually as a B-Complex) for people who are experiencing emotional distress consistently (Whitaker, 1995).

Antioxidant Vitamins, Minerals, and Herbs

Antioxidants are substances that prevent damage to the body from free radicals. Free radicals are molecules that are very reactive and bind to body tissue and damage it. This damage is called oxidation. Cut an apple in half and let it sit on your counter for an hour. When you return, you will see evidence of oxidation—the once white apple has turned brown. That is what happens to one's body when it is not protected sufficiently with antioxidant nutrients.

Research has shown that free radicals are responsible (at least in part) for causing (and worsening) the two major health problems of our day—heart disease and cancer. While much of the attention with heart disease has been on cholesterol, some research suggests that cholesterol is more likely to do its damage to artery walls if it (the cholesterol) is first altered by free radicals. Therefore, protecting cholesterol and arteries from free radical damage is important in the prevention of cardiovascular disease (Whitaker, 1995).

Our bodies are exposed to free radicals daily from both internal and external sources. Free radicals are the byproducts of many normal body processes that we cannot avoid. However, we can reduce our exposure to many sources of free radicals, such as alcohol, cigarettes, second-hand cigarette smoke, electrical fields (including electric blankets), pollution, fried foods, and stress. "Emotional stress" causes a reaction from one's body that produces a large amount of free radicals. This is why, most researchers believe, stress affects our body. If you look at someone who tends to be anxious and smokes regularly, he or she will usually look somewhat older than his or her same-aged peers. Just as they turn the apple brown, fee radicals seem to affect our skin by causing wrinkles.

The main antioxidant nutrients are Vitamins C and E. While we get these nutrients from the foods we eat, the amount we receive in our food is not enough to protect us from free radicals. Therefore, most holistic health practitioners recommend taking antioxidant supplements (usually 500 milligrams of Vitamin C and 400 international units of Vitamin E) daily and avoiding sources of free radicals (Whitaker, 1995).

Omega-3 Fatty Acids

Omega-3 fatty acids have become popular in recent years for their positive effects on the cardiovascular system and their apparent ability to raise HDL ("good") cholesterol. However, omega-3 fatty acids also appear to improve our emotional health as well.

Omega-3 fatty acids are effective in treating symptoms of depression in patients who remain depressed despite being on standard antidepressant medication therapy (Peet & Horrobin, 2002). In fact, Schmidt (1997) reports that omega-3 fatty acids can raise a natural antidepressant brain chemical called "dopamine" by 40 percent!

The two most popular sources of omega-3 fatty acids are fish and flax oil. While my preferred way of obtaining omega-3 fatty acids is through flax seed oil capsules, flax oil is helpful *in the brain* for only about one-third of us (Ross, 2002).

Ross (2002) recommends two grams of fish oil supplements a day.

Natural Help for Depressive Symptoms

Note that the following natural substances are not substitutes for learning the rational self-counseling skills detailed in this book! They can, though, be helpful in providing relief from depressive symptoms.

L-tyrosine

L-tyrosine is an amino acid (a building block of protein). While clinical studies (Werbach, 1991) have demonstrated L-tyrosine's effectiveness at reducing symptoms of depression, it is particularly helpful in reducing the potential side effects of antidepressants drugs known as SSRI's (Selective Serotonin Reuptake Inhibitors). Commonly prescribed SSRI's include:

SSRI Antidepressants

Prozac	Cipramil
Seromex	Emocal
Seronil	Sepram (Generic: Citalopram)
Fontex (Generic: Fluoxetine)	LuvoxFevarin (Generic: Fluvoxamine)
Paxil	Lexapro (Generic: Escitalopram)
Seroxat	Wellburtin (Generic: Bupropion)
OpitarAropax (Generic: Paroxetine)	Effexor (Generic: Venlafaxine)
Celexa	Zoloft (Generic: Sertroline).

L-tyrosine helps with the common SSRI side-effect of low energy (Korf et al., 1983). Serotonin is a neurotransmitter that is the biochemical counterbalance to your brain's natural stimulants, the catecholamines. Physicians prescribe SSRI antidepressants to raise serotonin levels in the patient's brain. **However, raising serotonin levels via SSRI's can deplete levels of catecholamines by as much as 60%.** The result of this decrease in catecholamines is low energy, apathy, twitches, tics, and sexual dysfunction.

According to Julia Ross (2002), L-tyrosine appears to restore the balance by improving the level of catecholamines. She recommends a dosage of 500 to 1000 milligrams to be taken in the morning to mid-afternoon (by 3:00 p.m.). Amino acids are best absorbed on an empty stomach.

Make certain to discuss L-tyrosine with your physician, especially if you are experiencing SSRI-induced side-effects. Also note that there is a possible negative interaction between L-tyrosine and MAO inhibitors (another type of antidepressant).

St. John's Wort

St. John's Wort is a well-researched herb with antidepressant properties. It has been found to be just as effective as Prozac for mild-moderate symptoms of depression (Schrader, 2000) and more effective than Zoloft for mild-moderate depressive symptoms (Brenner et al, 2000). Another benefit of St. John's Wort is that it appears to have antiviral properties.

The recommended dosage (Ross, 2002; Whitaker, 1995) is 300 mg, three times a day. Hypericum is the active antidepressive ingredient in St. John's Wort, so make certain that the supplement states on its packaging that it is standardized at .3% Hypericum.

Make certain to discuss St. John's Wort with your physician before taking it. Known interactions include birth control pills (it decreases the effectiveness of oral contraceptives), blood thinners (St. John's Wort thins the blood as well), and other antidepressants. It can also make a person sensitive to sunlight.

5-HTP

Supplementation with 5-HTP can provide rapid improvement in mood, sometimes within a matter of hours (Ross, 2002). Its ability to raise serotonin levels is what makes 5-HTP a potent antidepressant. In fact, the manufacturer of Prozac, Eli Lilly, conducted a study in which they combined 5-HTP with Prozac. Serotonin activity was increased by 150 percent with Prozac, but it increased to 650 percent when 5-HTP was added!

Another study comparing 5-HTP to the powerful antidepressant Luvox found that 5-HTP improved depressive symptoms in 68 percent of patients compared to 62 percent of those on Luvox (Poldinger et al, 1991).

Ross (2002) recommends starting with 50 milligrams in mid-afternoon. Add another 50 milligrams in an hour, if you do not receive much benefit. If needed, add a third 50 milligrams for maximum effect one hour later. Whichever level provided the desired result, repeat the dose at 9:30 p.m. (50-150 milligrams).

As for safety and side-effects, 5-HTP is associated with 0 percent sexual dysfunction (Benkert, 1976, 1975) while SSRI antidepressants are associated with 50-70 percent sexual dysfunction. Other studies (Ross, 2002) have shown that 5-HTP has had fewer side effects than the placebos! Of course, discuss 5-HTP supplementation with your physician before using it. There is a possible negative interaction with MAO inhibitors.

Natural Help for Anxiety Symptoms

Although medical science has developed very potent drugs that reduce symptoms of anxiety, there is a significant price to pay for using most of them—addiction! The following natural substances are nonaddictive and can be very potent as well. Be certain to discuss these substances with your physician before taking them, especially if you are taking psychiatric medications already, or are taking any medication that causes drowsiness, such as beta-blockers for the heart or antihistamines for allergies.

Calcium

Calcium is a muscle relaxer and pain reliever. It helps to produce general relaxation and can encourage sleep in those who have suffered from insomnia. While many claims have been made about the superiority of certain types or brands of calcium, they essentially are all the same. Ross (2002) recommends 500–1000 milligrams daily. Again, seek physician approval before beginning calcium supplementation.

Also note that supplemental calcium might interfere with the absorption of other nutrients and with medication. Therefore, take calcium at least four hours before or after taking medication or vitamins.

GABA

GABA (gamma-aminobutyric acid) has been described as your brain's natural Valium (Ross, 2002). Valium is a well-known anti-anxiety medication. In fact, Valium, along with other anti-anxiety medications, was designed to mimic or amplify GABA's naturally calming effects.

GABA is both an amino acid and an inhibitory neurotransmitter. It decreases production of adrenaline. Adrenaline is a hormone that causes the increase in heart rate, breathing rate, and nervousness we experience when something threatening confronts us. GABA supplementation can help turn off stress after we upset ourselves, and it can help prevent stressful responses when taken before an expected ordeal.

Ross (2002) recommends taking 500-1000 milligrams, one to three times a day. Again, talk with your doctor before taking GABA.

Valerian Root

Valerian Root is a rather foul-smelling herb that packs quite a calming punch. It is an excellent anti-anxiety agent with a very good safety profile (Bloomfield, 1998). One Utah woman in 1995 attempted suicide by taking twenty times the recommended dose of valerian root. She was discharged from the hospital the next day unharmed.

Valerian root is also very good for inducing sleep, and it as appears to decrease the incidence of nightmares.

As a sedative, Bloomfield (1998) recommends 300-900 milligrams taken one hour before bedtime. For general anxiety relief, the effects are dose-dependent. Therefore, follow the manufacturer's directions on the label until the desired effects are produced.

Chamomile

Chamomile is another excellent, safe anti-anxiety herb (Bloomfield, 1998). This herb is ingested most often in form of tea.

Besides its excellent anti-anxiety properties, chamomile is an antispasmodic and can help alleviate menstrual cramps. Chamomile also is very effective in treating gastrointestinal discomfort, including nausea. A warm cup of chamomile tea before going to bed can help you to fall asleep.

Again, the effects of chamomile are dose-dependent. You might need to experiment to determine whether using one or two tea bags produce the desired effect. On a cautionary note, avoid chamomile if you have a ragweed allergy. Also, do not use chamomile for more than seven consecutive days as a ragweed allergy might result.

Sometimes Allergies Cause Psychiatric Symptoms

Dr. William Crook's book, *Solving the Puzzle of Your Hard-To-Raise Child,* "should be" required reading for all mental health professionals. In his book, Dr. Crook clearly establishes the fact that allergies can, and often do, cause a host of symptoms that are often mistakenly believed to be indicative of a psychiatric disorder.

Crook (1987) suggests that allergies (both food and airborne) cause symptoms of anxiety (psychomotor agitation, vertigo, nausea, confusion), symptoms of depression (fatigue, lethargy), and neurological symptoms, like ticks, tremors, and Tourette's Syndrome. Allergies also can cause inattention and hyperactivity, and encourage the misbehavior that often coincides.

According to Crook, symptoms of allergies include:

–a pale color
–dark circles under the eyes (allergic "shiners")
–a congested nose
–allergic gape (person tends to keep the mouth open because the nose is stuffed)
–headaches (especially in the forehead)
–fatigue or drowsiness
–inability to concentrate
–short attention span
–hyperactivity
–nausea or other stomach discomfort
–muscle aches.

These symptoms can give a person the impression that he or she is depressed, anxious, or both. Considering these symptoms is important, especially if it seems to you that you are depressed or anxious, but are not particularly upset about anything.

If you experience these symptoms, ask your physician about getting tested and treated (if necessary) for allergies. Even if you are reacting to something in your life, and that is what encouraged you to enter therapy, allergies might be making matters worse for you.

Sleep

Anyone that has ever been around a person who consistently loses sleep knows the main effect of it—fatigue, irritation, and anger! Sound sleep is a necessary part of good mental and physical health. Without it, many physical problems can develop. The resultant fatigue makes otherwise small problems seem catastrophic as the person simply does not have the energy to handle things well.

Many people think that they do not have to take their sleep schedule seriously. But sleeping recharges our batteries, so to speak. Just like an electronic device, eventually we too slow down and stop when our batteries get too low.

Often, people have difficulty sleeping when they have excessive worries or fears. They might have difficulty falling asleep. They might wake up intermittently throughout the night. Often, they experience both.

To get quality sleep:

(1) make certain that you get between six and eight hours per night;

(2) maintain a regular sleep schedule so that your body will know it's time to sleep;

(3) realize that there is no point in thinking about your concerns in the middle of the night unless you can do something about them then. So allow yourself to be distracted by something else, like music, until you fall asleep.

(4) with your physician's approval, make use of chamomile or valerian root to help you sleep soundly, naturally.

Exercise

Exercise can be very beneficial to improving one's emotional state in several different ways. First, exercise helps your body release several different hormones and other chemicals that produce a sense of energy and well-being. Conversely, *not* exercising or being otherwise physically active can produce the opposite effect—lethargy, apathy, and depression. We all have had days that we spent watching television or "lying around." We often feel much greater fatigue during those days than we do during days in which we engaged in physical activity.

Second, exercise helps "burn away" the chemical byproducts of anxiety and depression that would otherwise take their toll on our organs. Third, when we make exercise fun, it gives us something to which we can look forward. I recommend light daily exercise with your physician's approval. Ask your doctor to recommend an exercise program that is best for you. Find an exercise partner or two and begin a weight-training program, or join an aerobics class, or simply go for a leisurely stroll. It's a great way to socialize and take care of your body and mind at the same time.

Blumenthal (1999) and his colleagues surprised many people when they demonstrated that regular exercise is as effective as antidepressant medications for patients who are depressed. The researchers studied 156 older adults diagnosed with major depression, assigning them to receive the antidepressant Zoloft, 30 minutes of exercise three times a week, or both. According to Blumenthal,

"Our findings suggest that a modest exercise program is an effective, robust treatment for patients with major depression who are positively inclined to participate in it. The benefits of exercise are likely to endure particularly among those who adopt it as a regular, ongoing life activity."

Blumenthal (2000) and his colleagues continued to follow the same subjects for six additional months and found that the group who exercised, but did not receive Zoloft, did better than either of the other two groups.

Exercise (especially weight training) can also enhance confidence. The increase in strength and stamina often results in a greater perception of being able to handle problems as they come our way.

Refrain from excessive alcohol, tobacco, and caffeine use

Alcohol is a central nervous system depressant. If you are already depressed or otherwise sluggish, alcohol can make you feel worse. Granted, many people try to make themselves feel better by getting drunk. However, the good feeling of being intoxicated is often replaced with a hangover, fatigue, and possible social, legal, and work-related problems as well. It is in your best interest to have all of your resources available to you to deal with your problems. Drinking alcohol excessively only interferes with your ability to take care of business.

Avoid tobacco and caffeine if you are experiencing anxiety consistently. Using these two substances when anxious is like pouring gasoline onto a fire. Cigarette smoking produces carbon monoxide, a gas that robs your body of oxygen. Whenever we are deprived of oxygen, we feel lethargic. Cigarette smoking also produces cyanide—the gas used in "gas chambers." An excellent resource for smoking cessation is my program, "The Drug-Free Smoking Cure®" which can be ordered from the National Association of Cognitive-Behavioral Therapists (1-800-853-1135).

Routine

In the late 1960's, Holmes and Rahe (1967) undertook a series of stress management studies to determine what events in life cause the greatest stress effects. Because of this research they concluded that it may be possible to anticipate stress crises and assist people in overcoming their stress.

Homes and Rahe had research subjects rate common life events by "Life Crisis Units" (LCU's) and then ranked their responses. This is how the subjects responded:

Event	LCU's	Event	LCU's
Death of spouse	100	Change in responsibilities at work	29
Divorce	73	Son or daughter leaving home	29
Separation	65	Trouble with in-laws	29
Jail term	63	Outstanding personal achievement	28
Death of close family member	63	Spouse begins or stops work	26
Personal illness or injury	53	Begin or end of school or college	26
Marriage	50	Change in living conditions	25
Fired at work	47	Change in personal habits	24
Marital reconciliation	45	Trouble with boss	23
Retirement	45	Change in work hours or conditions	20
Change in health of family member	44	Change in residence	20
Pregnancy	40	Change in school or college	20
Sex difficulties	39	Change in recreation	19
Gain of new family member	39	Change in church activities	19
Business readjustment	38	Change in social activities	18
Change in financial state	38	A moderate loan or mortgage	17
Death of close friend	37	Change in sleeping habits	16
Change to a different line of work	36	Change in number of family get-togethers	15
Change in number of arguments with spouse	35	Change in eating habits	15
A large mortgage or loan	30	Holiday	13
Foreclosure of mortgage or loan	30	Christmas	12
		Minor violations of law	11

Ranking of Amount of Change Produced by Various Life Events (Holmes & Ruch, 1971)

Homes and Rahe defined stress as the body's adaptation to change. The more that a person has to adapt to a life event, the more stress the body experiences. It does not matter as much whether the life event is viewed as positive (like getting married) or negative (like getting divorced) as it does the amount of adaptation required to adjust to the event. In other words, it usually takes more time adjusting to getting married than it does to getting a traffic ticket.

Homes and Rahe discovered that the likelihood of people developing physical illness varies with how much change they experience in a given time frame. The more stress one experiences, the greater is the likelihood that one will experience a physical illness.

The human body thrives on regularity, and it attempts to adapt to change. Whether the change is seen as being good (winning one million dollars) or bad (death of one's spouse), the body must adapt to it regardless.

Even minor changes in one's daily routine causes stress. Going to work a different route is stressful. Waking up at different times is stressful. Therefore, the more *irregularity* we have in our daily living, the more stress we experience.

I encourage you to maintain a regular schedule of sleeping, eating, exercising, bathing, working, relaxing, and anything else you do regularly. Your body will thank you for it. Feeling good physically will make it easier to feel good emotionally.

2

Factors Affecting Progress in Therapy

"If you always do what you've always done,
You will always get what you have always gotten…"

Sometimes certain attitudes slow progress in therapy, such as fears of changing, doubts about one's ability to change, and biological and environmental factors. In this chapter, I will describe some of the most common reasons people do not progress as quickly as they could. I will also explain how to overcome these factors.

While it is possible that you will read this chapter and find nothing that relates to you, if anything in this chapter relates to you in any way, be sure to mark it so that you can discuss it with your therapist during your next session.

Attitude: "I do not want therapy."

This is an attitude often expressed by clients who have the perception that they are being forced to receive mental health treatment. When clients tell me that they do not want therapy, I explain that no one does—not because therapy is unpleasant, but because *therapy* is not the thing to be desired (or "wanted"). Therapy helps us get what we really want.

However, sometimes people unintentionally confuse themselves by thinking that they have to *want* to do something to *do* it. We do many things that we really do not want to do (like going to work), but we want what we get from doing them (like money).

We use this logic when helping people with habit control problems, such as cigarette smoking. Many people believe, "You have to *want* to quit smoking to quit." If that were the case, rarely would anyone ever stop smoking. What most people who smoke *want* is to be able to smoke and not suffer the consequences. People quit smoking when they realize that they want something more than cigarettes.

If you are focusing on "not wanting therapy," it most likely means that both your goals (what you want out of life) and the idea that therapy can help you achieve those goals, are not clearly established. Your therapist can help you with both. Obviously, if you can consistently get what you want out of life without therapy, terrific! But if there is something that your therapist can share with you that will make it easier or more likely that you will achieve your goals, why not let him or her share it with you?

Cognitive-Emotive Dissonance and Gut Thinking

Cognitive-Emotive Dissonance is the strange feeling that we feel in our gut (where we feel our emotions) when we do something, think something, or feel something that is the opposite of that to which we are accustomed. It feels strange. It "feels wrong."

For example, if you were to place a pen in the opposite hand with which you write and tried to write with that hand, not only would you not write well, but it would feel strange and wrong. This "wrong" feeling is called cognitive-emotive dissonance.

Cognitive-emotive dissonance is **unavoidable**—we will experience it *anytime* we do something, think something, feel something, or are exposed to something that is the opposite of that to which we are accustomed.

People experience many changes that create cognitive-emotive dissonance. Examples include:

–living on your own after being married for twenty years,

–eating a vegetarian diet after eating meat all of your life,

–moving into a new home,

–working for a new employer,

–feeling happy when you've felt depressed for years,

–asserting yourself when you have been accustomed to keeping quiet,

–having money when you have been accustomed to being poor,

–thinking that you are smart when all of your life you thought that you were not,

–going to a different church, or changing religions,

–someone treating you well when you have been consistently mistreated.

These are examples of situations from which we expect to experience cognitive-emotive dissonance.
"Gut Thinking" is the mistaken idea that our emotional feelings are proof that what we are thinking is correct. According to "gut thinking,"

if it *feels* wrong, it must *be* wrong;

if it *feels* right, it must *be* right;

if I *feel* afraid, I *must* be in a dangerous situation;

if I *feel* depressed, my situation *must* really be as bad as I'm feeling.

However, the only thing that our emotional feelings prove is that we are thinking something to create them. Our feelings do not prove that we are right or wrong, that our situation is good or bad. Our feelings only prove that we are thinking something to create them. Therefore,

just because it *feels* wrong *doesn't* mean it is wrong;

just because it *feels* right *doesn't* mean it is right;

just because I *feel* afraid *doesn't* mean that I must be in a dangerous situation;

just because if I *feel* depressed *doesn't* mean that my situation *is* really that bad

What does this have to do with therapy? Some of what your therapist shares with you will feel strange and wrong. Changing your behavior and emotions will feel strange and wrong. Adopting a different lifestyle or different living arrangement will feel strange and wrong. If you were to think, "Since it feels wrong, it must be wrong," you would immediately refuse it.

The only thing that this "wrong" feeling proves is that you are not accustomed to the new way of thinking, feeling, and acting. The only thing that rids us of cognitive-emotive dissonance is practice. The more we practice the new ideas, behaviors, and feelings, the sooner they will feel "right." The more we write with the pen in our non-preferred hand, the sooner writing with that hand will feel "right" to us.

Immediate negative reactions to information presented in therapy could be the result of cognitive-emotive dissonance. ***Therefore, give new ideas a chance!***

For example, I remember one day sitting in my living room watching television with a picture of a balcony on the screen. After several minutes a man came walking out. It was the new pope, Pope Benedict XVI. My immediate reaction was, "I don't like him." The man had not yet uttered a single word, but I already had a negative reaction to him. Therefore, I asked myself, "Aldo, why do you not like him?" Asking myself that question helped me to realize that what I was experiencing was cognitive-emotive dissonance. For the previous twenty-six years, another man, Pope John Paul II walked out onto that balcony. Seeing another man do so felt strange and wrong, therefore giving me the immediate impression that it *was* wrong. I therefore encouraged myself to give him a chance.

Healthy, Normal Resistance

When is it actually healthy and normal for clients to resist suggestions given by therapists? When therapists are wrong, for example! How could a therapist be wrong? Therapists can make an incorrect assessment of the client. Sometimes therapists are mistaken about the severity of the client's problem or concerning what the client's problem actually is. Most often, though, if a therapist is incorrect, it will be concerning the cause of the client's problem.

Anytime two people communicate with each other there is a chance for misunderstanding, and that fact applies to therapeutic communication as well.

If it seems to you that your therapist is not on the right track (based on what he or she is saying or suggesting to you), make certain to share your perception with him or her. A good therapist will not take offense or be upset in any way with your honesty. Your therapist's goal is to help you achieve your goals, not to have you agree with everything that he or she says. In fact, if I am wrong in some way about my client, I hope that he or she lets me know!

Fear of Discomfort

The fear of discomfort is one of the strongest forms of resistance in therapy. It is based on the idea that feeling upset is unbearable. The client's thought that feeling upset is unbearable leads him or her to avoid anything that would cause upset feelings, such as talking about certain problems. As a result, sometimes clients are very reluctant to discuss important issues, and, therefore, have a difficult time getting better.

If you are reluctant to discuss certain issues because you are concerned that you will feel upset, the next topic, "symptom stress" will be very important to you.

Symptom Stress

Besides feeling upset about a situation, many people also end up feeling upset about the fact that they are upset! Dr. Albert Ellis (2002) calls this "symptom stress." Examples of symptoms stress include:

–being depressed about being depressed,
–being anxious about being depressed,
–being depressed about being anxious,
–being anxious about being anxious,
–being afraid that you are going insane,
–being afraid that you are going to have a nervous breakdown,
–being afraid that you are losing your mind,

–being afraid that you will need to be hospitalized,
–being afraid that you will always have your problem,
–putting yourself down for not having resolved your problem,
–putting yourself down for being the only one with your particular problem.

There are three main reasons why Rational Living Therapists and other cognitive-behavioral therapists concern themselves with symptom stress. First, we do not have an endless supply of energy (although many of us have much more energy than we think we do). If we use a significant amount of our energy being upset about the fact that we are upset, that does not leave much energy to deal with the reason we were upset to being with!

Second, symptom stress can distract a person significantly. I have met many people who were so caught up with the fact that they were upset that they actually forgot the original reason they were upset!

Third, symptom stress puts undo pressure on the client, giving him or her the impression that relief must be obtained immediately. This insistence on immediate relief often leads people to engage in very irrational behavior (drinking alcohol, taking drugs, excessive gambling) to obtain that "needed" relief.

The most common belief that causes symptom stress is,

"I can't stand how I feel!"

When people tell me that they cannot stand feeling depressed, anxious, angry, or otherwise upset, I know that their belief is incorrect. Obviously they *can stand it* because if they couldn't, it would have killed them.

When I mention this fact to therapists that I train, sometimes they tell me, "Oh Aldo, that's just playing with words. When people say that they can't stand how they feel, they really don't mean that it will kill them." Keep in mind, though, that when it comes to our emotions and behavior, it's not just semantics (words), it's all semantics (Maultsby, 1984).

Keep three important facts in mind. First, in relation to our emotions and behavior, the human brain is our humble servant (Maultsby, 1984). It does not care what we think. It allows us to think whatever we want, whether the thought is accurate or not.

Second, the human body does not lie (if it is working properly). In other words, the human body will provide the brain the logical response to what is thought in the brain. If a person thinks a depressing thought, the body will respond with depression. If a person thinks a fearful thought, the body will react with anxiety.

Third, there are three types of statements we make to ourselves—jokes, lies, and sincere statements. If a person is just joking or lying when making the statement, "I can't stand how I feel," that statement will not have much of an emotional effect.

However, how do we react when we have the *sincere* belief that we cannot stand how we feel? We react as if we were in a life-or-death situation, like being in a burning building. That is the reaction I see in people when they sincerely believe that they cannot stand their emotional feelings. Since the body does not lie, we know that this reaction must be the result of equating feeling upset with something that could kill the person.

Since no person has ever died as the direct result of being upset, I encourage my clients to change the statement, "I can't stand how I feel," to,

"I don't like how I have been feeling, and since I do not like it, I'm working to make myself feel the way I want to feel. Until then, I can stand feeling this way."

Emotional distress is unpleasant, uncomfortable, and unfortunate, but it is something that we all can tolerate or "stand!" Realizing this makes people feel much less pressure to get better, and actually speeds their progress.

If you have concerns about your condition, discuss them with your therapist. Keep in mind that being upset about your emotional condition serves no useful purpose and actually makes it harder for you to feel better. Realize that you are in the process of learning to feel better, and through time and diligent practice, you will feel better. *Refuse* to distract yourself with unproductive thoughts about how you are feeling and work on imagining how good you will feel when you are feeling as good as you want to feel. Also, realize that:

–most mental health clients are not in need of hospitalization (and it's not the end of the world for those that do);

–no person has ever lost his or her mind;

–there is no such thing as a nervous breakdown (if there were, you would need a neurologist, not a psychiatrist!);

–people with healthy brains (the overwhelming majority of mental health clients) have control over their emotions. Because of that fact, we need not worry that we will be "stuck" uncontrollably in a depressive or anxious state;

–the reason most people fear that they will always have their problem is because it *seems* that way given the fact that they do not know how to rid themselves of the problem. Just because it seems that way does not make it so;

–most people's problems are a matter of degree, not kind. What I mean is that what they are experiencing is not unique or different than what everyone experiences, but that it might be more severe. For example, everyone experiences depression at times, but maybe not to the degree that would require hospitalization. However, most people do not experience hallucinations (seeing or hearing things that are not actually there). When people experience hallucinations consistently, that is a problem that is different in kind;

–You cannot fix something if you do not know how to do so. We do not expect ourselves to know how to do brain surgery, yet we expect to be able to counsel ourselves rationally about a particular situation before we have actually learned how. Society certainly doesn't teach us how to think properly. Our parents do not teach us how to deal with situations in a rational manner (because they do not know themselves). Rational self-counseling is not taught in school. Therefore, it is highly unrealistic to expect that you would know how to make yourself feel better when you are feeling down. Actually, I wonder how people do as well as they do given what they learn growing up;

–people do not walk around with signs saying, "I suffer from severe depression," or "I abuse my children," or "I worry about everything," or "I had an abortion two years ago." Because people can act "normally" although they are quite upset "inside," it makes it seem as though no one else has your problem but you.

Fear of Disclosure and Shame

Sometimes people have done things, thought things, or had desires for things for which they are ashamed. They know it would be a good idea to share this information with their therapist since it is a part of the reason they have sought therapy. However, sometimes people are very reluctant to share this "shameful" information with their therapist fearing that the therapist might react negatively or no longer accept them.

Cognitive-behavioral therapists are taught to *unconditionally* accept clients as human beings, no matter what clients admit to us. Our goal is to help you, not judge you! Therapists hear many things in the course of their career, so it is unlikely that what you share with your therapist will be anything that the therapist has not heard before (or at least a variation of it).

Also keep in mind that therapists are not mind-readers. Sometimes clients think that if they hint around enough about their "shameful" problems, the therapist will eventually realize what they are without the client needing to state them directly. This strategy is very inefficient and most often ineffective.

Therapists understand that establishing a trusting relationship with their clients is important. It is understandable that a person would be reluctant to share personal information with a complete stranger. When you feel comfortable sharing personal information, I encourage you to do so. Keep in mind, though, that your goal in seeking therapy is to achieve your life goals, *not* to have your therapist's approval. So refuse to overly concern yourself with the therapist's possible reaction, and refuse to let any reaction stand in your way of achieving your goals.

Therapeutic Hopelessness

"I can't change. I can't get better. There is no hope for me." If I were in therapy and I thought that way, I probably would not put much effort into it. Actually, I do not know why I would be in therapy if I thought that way.

Therapeutic hopelessness is often the result of past therapeutic failures. "I've been to several therapists. I've tried many things, and I'm still not better, so there must be something wrong with me. I must not have the potential to get better."

This attitude is based on the general mistaken belief,

"Because I haven't, that proves I can't."

People apply this belief to many different kinds of goals. *However, the only thing that a lack of progress in therapy proves is that what is necessary to experience progress has not yet been done! It does not prove that the client has a lack of potential, or that the therapy was poor. When we look at it in these terms, it opens our mind to ask ourselves, "What are those necessary ingredients that have been missing?"*

Many clients tell me, "I don't think I'll ever get over being depressed, because I have tried for years to feel better, and I just haven't…" After asking them the methods they have used to feel better, it becomes obvious why they continue to be miserable—their *methods would be unsuccessful for anyone!* In other words, they do not know proven, effective methods to make themselves feel better! When they begin learning rational self-counseling skills, they quickly realize that they *do* have the potential to feel happy.

Therefore,

"Just because you haven't doesn't mean you can't!"

In my opinion, "hopelessness" is the wrong term for the experience. A person is always free to hope, no matter how bad their situation appears! A better, more accurate term is "irrational pessimism."

Hopelessness, or irrational pessimism, is based on the assumption, "I know all that there is to know about this problem. Since *I* do not see a solution to the problem, a solution must not exist." This assumption is irrational because it assumes that nothing exists outside of what we know. However, no one knows all there is to know about anything. Even so-called experts only know what they know, God only knows what they do not know. Therefore, refuse to accept an "expert's" proclamation that your situation is "hopeless."

As long as your goals are important to you, continue researching the topic. Conducting research has never been easier than it is today. Type any word on a search engine on the Internet, and once you get past the pornography, you will find information associated with that word of which you were completely unaware. So continue searching for a solution. Why not? What do you have to lose?

If at some point a goal is no longer important, stop searching. Otherwise, go for it!

Fear of Success

Sounds strange, doesn't it? A fear of *success*? Why would someone be afraid to succeed at something at which they are wanting to succeed?

Usually, a fear of success is really of fear of subsequent failure. It is a concern that if one achieves a goal, he or she might fail to maintain that progress. Sometimes it is a concern that changing will lead to a worse situation than a person has already.

Sometimes a fear of success gives others the impression that a person does not *want* to change or succeed, when in fact there is desire, but the fear of what might happen if the person were to change prevents the change.

Some common fears that I have heard include:

–I won't know what to do with myself in the evening if I don't drink;

–I'll lose my friends if I stop drinking;

–If people see me walking with a limp, they will think something is wrong with me;

–If I start feeling happy, I'm afraid I won't be able to keep feeling that way;

–If I feel better, people might start expecting things from me;

–If I act differently, I won't really be me anymore;

–If I think that I could make it on my own, I would *have to* leave my husband, because I would be out of my mind to stay with him if I knew that I didn't have to.

Many thoughts can make a person reluctant to change, even though he or she wants to change. Thankfully, most often these fears are unfounded. What is feared either is not likely to happen, or a person actually could cope with it if it were to happen. If you have any fear or reluctance to change your thinking, feelings, or behavior, be certain to discuss your concerns with your therapist.

Resisting Therapy

Some clients, especially those who are court-ordered or who are seeking therapy at the insistence of someone else, have the sincere, but mistaken impression that they are *forced* to attend their therapy sessions. This perception of being forced causes a person to resent participating in therapy, and often leads them to refuse to do so. When this is the case, I point out to clients the difference between *force* and *choice*. A typical scenario is:

Client: "I hate that I'm forced to come to therapy."

Me: "What gives you the impression that you are forced to come to therapy?"

Client: "The judge said that if I do not come to therapy, I'm going to jail."

Me: "Well, it sounds to me like you have a choice. You could either come to therapy and avoid jail, or refuse to come to therapy and go to jail. Granted, I'll bet that you think both choices stink, and that you'd rather spend the same amount of time in the Bahamas. Please realize, though, that just because you do not have a pleasant choice does not mean that you do not have a choice. In fact, the only way a person could be forced to come to therapy is if he or she were transported against his or her will."

Client: "What difference does any of this make?"

Me: "Anytime we think that we are being forced to do something that we do not want to do, we resent the heck out of it. The more we resent it, the more time we spend resisting it. It is much more difficult to significantly resent doing something that we realize that we are actively *choosing* or *deciding* to do, even if we do not like doing it. Secondly, many people do not have much faith in their ability to make good, rational decisions for themselves. If you think that the "judge" is making you attend therapy, you are not going to give yourself credit for having made the wise decision to attend therapy instead of going to jail."

Another statement that I hear sometimes from clients is, "You're not going to tell me what to do." Clients making this statement are absolutely correct. Rational Living Therapists are not in the business of telling people how to live their lives. We do not impose our values, morals, or goals on our clients. We do not tell people *what* to do, we show people *how* to do based on what they want. That's why we take the time to discover what our clients want out of life.

Self-Punishment

Sometimes people do things that they later regret, and they think that they somehow must be punished for what they have done. A typical guilt-inducing belief is, "Because I've committed an evil act, that makes me a rotten person that *must* suffer, that doesn't deserve to benefit from therapy and to be happy." This belief is irrational for several reasons, so let's examine them.

First, it's important for a person to examine how much he or she *actually* is responsible for the undesirable event that has occurred. Sometimes people blame themselves for negative situations when in fact it was not their fault. Other times a person is only partially responsible. There is no point in attributing the cause of a negative event to oneself more than actually is the case.

Second, there is no such thing as a "rotten person." What actually exists, though, are people who do "rotten" things. While some people are more inclined than others, we are all capable of doing "rotten" things.

Third, it is a problem to believe that one *must* suffer, even if one is completely responsible for causing a very undesirable situation. If a person were to tell me that she *wanted* to suffer, I would respond by saying, "That's your business. You are entitled to suffer as much as you care to." I might point out the disadvantages of suffering, but as long as the motivation to suffer is only a "want," who am I to tell people that they are not allowed to suffer? There is a big difference, though, between *wanting* to suffer and thinking that one *must* suffer. When people believe that they must suffer, I encourage them to look at the evidence. What evidence is there that a person absolutely must suffer for committing an act that is wrong?

Sometimes people believe that they must suffer because they believe that their religion tells them to do so. When that is the case, I refer my clients to their priest, minister, rabbi—someone that is an expert on their approach to religion to make certain that they have the facts straight. Most people, after having met with their religious leader, learn that there is no requirement that a person damn himself or herself for eternity. However, sometimes a person's religion does require endless suffering in response to committing a "sin." In those cases, I point out to the client that he or she has every right in the world to continue practicing the religion and making himself or herself miserable accordingly. On the other hand, I emphasize that the client also has every right in the world to look into other approaches to religion to see what they have to say about forgiveness. If this is a concern of yours, and you do not believe that you are free to research other approaches to religion, be certain to share your concern with your therapist.

Sometimes people think that they must suffer because others have told them so. Again, where is the evidence? Keep in mind that many rules are simply made up and are passed down through generations as if they were based on absolute fact. Even if a person were to believe that suffering is the "right" thing to do, who decided that this idea is correct, and based on what evidence?

When a person insists on suffering to some degree for having committed a sin, I ask them, "How long must you suffer?" Any answer given to this question will be arbitrary—in other words, made up. Even those who kill others do not necessarily receive a life sentence, yet many people sentence themselves to a lifetime of unhappiness until they learn that they do not need to do so.

Many people believe that suffering (damning oneself) is important to avoid repeating a problem behavior. They believe that if they punish themselves enough, they will be less likely to repeat the behavior. Punishing yourself is *not* required to avoid repeating a behavior. To avoid repeating a problem behavior, it is important to have a reason to refuse to repeat the behavior, a commitment to refuse to repeat the behavior, knowledge of how to refuse to repeat the behavior (and do something else instead), and acting on that knowledge.

If you have done something of which you are ashamed or about which you feel bad, accept that fact, learn from it, refuse to do it again, and move on with your life! Why not? You are not helping anyone or anything by refusing to be happy!

Client-Therapist Mismatching

Some people receiving counseling or psychotherapy have the impression that if their therapist is not similar to them in some way, the therapist could not develop an adequate understanding of their problem to help them. Clients sometimes believe that their therapist must share their same religious background, gender (sex), sexual orientation, or ethnic background. Other times, clients believe that therapists must have certain experiences to be helpful. When this is the case, therapists hear comments, like:

–"How could you teach me about parenting, if you do not have kids?";
–"What do you know about drug abuse, if you've never used drugs?";
–"You've never been to prison, so how can you help me cope with being in the pen?"

If you believe that your therapist does not understand your concerns, be certain to share your perception with him or her. However, I encourage you to give your therapist a chance to understand you. Express your thoughts, feelings, experiences, and concerns. Therapists cannot develop an exact understanding of a client's concerns and experiences, mostly because of the limitations of language and communication. Thankfully, a therapist does not need to develop an *exact* understanding, but rather an *adequate* understanding to be helpful.

We do not require our medical doctors to experience every illness for which they treat us. We tell the doctor what we are experiencing, the doctor makes a diagnosis, and based on his or her training, prescribes the appropriate treatment. How does the doctor know which is the appropriate treatment? Not by having experienced the same illness, but by studying it.

Mental health therapists spend a great deal of time studying peoples' problems and concerns. They also receive extensive training in how to listen so that they can develop a good understanding of their clients' concerns. Therefore, they also can "prescribe" the appropriate therapy for you without having experienced your problems or concerns.

I am not suggesting, though, that people do not have a right to seek a therapist with whom they would feel comfortable—certainly they do. You always have the right to seek the services of a different mental health professional if you are not satisfied with your current treatment provider.

An Unwillingness to Learn

Cognitive-behavioral therapy (Rational Living Therapy) is an educational approach to helping people feel the way they want to feel and to achieve their goals. An assumption of cognitive-behavioral therapy (that is based on a lot of research evidence) is that people will feel better, do better, and "get" better after they learn rational self-counseling skills. However, some people seeking therapy resist learning these skills. Three very common beliefs cause this unwillingness to learn.

1. "I shouldn't have to learn rational self-counseling skills." If I were to ask you, "What should 1 + 1 equal?", you would say, "Aldo, of course it should equal two." What if I were to say to you, though, that I want 1 + 1 to equal four, and that I'm going to hold my breath until it does? You would say to me that I'm going to look strange as I turn purple from holding my breath, because 1 + 1 will never equal four, no matter how much I think that it should (or want it to).

The same logic applies to our emotional and behavioral goals. No matter how much we wish that we would not need to learn rational self-counseling skills to feel better and do better *consistently*, the fact is, we do!

Now, we can do some things to make ourselves feel "better" temporarily that do not require much learning at all. Smoking crack cocaine does not require much learning. Drinking alcohol does not require much learning. Neither does popping a pill. However, those irrational attempts to feel better provide only temporary relief (and often create other problems). *To feel and do well consistently, on purpose, we need to learn how to do so.*

Cognitive-behavioral therapists/Rational Living Therapists understand that most people do not know the rational self-counseling skills that RLT teaches. There is a very good reason why most people are not familiar with these rational self-counseling skills—no one teaches them to us! The skills that your therapist will teach you are not taught to us growing up.

What *do* we learn growing up? If anything, we learn how to make ourselves miserable! We have many teachers (friends, family, school teachers, etc....) teaching us how to think and behave irrationally. We are surrounded with irrational messages, such as the nonsense that we hear in songs. Take, for example, one of the top music hits of the early 1970's, Harry Nilsson's *"Can't Live if Living is Without You."* This single sold many, many records, but what a highly irrational message!

I would imagine that if I were to record a song entitled, "I Love You, But I Don't Need You to Live" that my song would not sell even one CD (well, maybe *one*). Not very romantic, but very rational!

Fact is, we learn our emotions and behaviors using the same process by which we learn to read, write, type, drive, and virtually everything else that we do (Maultsby, 1984). So to feel the way we want to feel, consistently, intentionally, we must learn how to do so.

We all are free to reject learning rational self-counseling skills. There is a price to be paid, though, and that price is not experiencing long-term happiness.

2. **"I already know these skills."** Sometimes those receiving counseling, especially those who have been in therapy for a while with other therapists, think that they already know all there is to know about rational self-counseling. Because this is a sincere belief, some clients believe that it is a waste of time for their therapist to teach them these skills.

If you believe that you already know the skills taught by cognitive-behavioral therapists/Rational Living Therapists, look through the pages of this book. See if you can find anything that you might not know. If you do know all of the skills taught in this book, and you continue to feel unwanted emotional distress, it could be that you do not know how to apply those skills to your concerns. Ask your therapist to help you.

3. **"It's not going to help me anyway."** By asking you to learn the skills described in this book, your therapist, based on his or her training and experience, has concluded that you can learn them and that learning them will have a beneficial effect.

The decision to ask you to learn rational self-counseling skills is based on what you have told your therapist about why you are seeking therapy, your symptoms, and what you have been experiencing. Your therapist likely has seen other people with similar problems and concerns be helped by these skills. Your therapist also knows that scientific research proves that people benefit from learning these skills. Given these facts, why wouldn't your therapist suggest that you learn them?

Some clients believe that these rational self-counseling skills might help others, but not them. If you believe this to be the case for you, share your belief with your therapist. Ultimately, what I encourage you to consider is:

What do you have to lose?

What would you really lose if you were to spend the next few weeks reading the information in this book, allowing your therapist to share this information with you and to show you how to apply it to your concerns, and if you were to practice these skills, only to discover that it was not helpful to you at all? What would you lose, *really*? No one is asking you to invest any amount of time, money, or effort that is contrary to your well-being. Learning rational self-counseling is not like jumping out of an airplane without a parachute or walking on hot coals.

Also consider what you have to gain by discovering that learning rational self-counseling is helpful to you. What do you have to gain? Refer to the pages where you listed your goals—that is what you have to gain!

Suppression

Suppression is the most common coping method people use to feel better. For most people, suppression is the only conscious coping method they have. Suppression is focusing your attention away from something over which you are upset onto something that you are not. Common ways of suppressing include keeping busy, working long hours, drinking alcohol, smoking, concerning oneself with *others'* problems, television watching, reading, excessive gambling, and overeating. In other words, people use just about anything that will distract them to suppress.

Suppression seems like a good way of coping because almost immediate relief results from it. However, suppression is a coping method that is doomed to fail by design. First, the problem or concern continues to exist—most problems do not resolve themselves. Second, while we have complete control over *how* we think about something, we do not have complete control over *what* we think about at any given moment. Your second grade teacher. Do you remember your second grade teacher? How likely is it that you would have thought about your second grade teacher this very moment had I not asked you to?

This is precisely the experience that many clients who tend to suppress report. They will say something like, "All I know is that I was watching T.V. and feeling good, and then something came on the show that reminded me of the girlfriend who left me, and I was right back to feeling upset about it again!"

For this reason, cognitive-behavioral therapists/Rational Living Therapists encourage clients to think about their problems long enough to learn how to think differently about them and to practice the new thinking. This new thinking is designed to help the person feel (at worst) calm when reminded of the problem situation. Therefore, in the future, when the client is reminded of the problem situation, he or she will be much more willing to think about it and work on it.

Secondary Gain

Secondary gain is receiving benefit from having a problem. Sometimes having a problem gets a person something that they want (their spouse's affection) or removes something that a person does not want (responsibility).

Secondary gain can be a great motivator to hold on to a problem. For example, a wife might notice that the only time her husband pays attention to her is when she is depressed. Because she believes she needs his attention, she intentionally or, perhaps, unintentionally resists measures that would make her feel better.

The benefits of secondary gain are often not really thought about consciously, but they remain motivators nonetheless. Without realizing it, a father's anxiety might bring about a calming of family conflict because the family members do not want to "upset dad." Therefore, the benefits of the family peace help to maintain the anxiety, even if the anxiety's cause had nothing to do with family conflict.

Secondary gain usually is based on one of two mistaken beliefs: "The only way to get what I want or need is to have a problem" or "The easier way to get what I want or need is to have a problem, and it makes sense to go the easier route." Let's examine these two ideas.

"The *only* way for me to get what I want or need is to have a problem." We certainly want to challenge this belief, because I cannot think of a single time when this belief was accurate. Is it indeed the case that the only way a person's spouse would be willing to provide attention and affection is if he were to remain depressed? Might the client's spouse enjoy providing attention and affection if the client were to satisfy the spouse's desires?

If you believe that you must hold onto your emotional state or behaviors because you need them to obtain what you want or need, obviously you believe that you are correct, or you would not waste your time feeling and behaving that way. However, I urge you to challenge that belief. Share this belief with your therapist, and allow him or her to work with you.

"The easier way to get what I want or need is to have a problem, and it makes sense to go the easier route." Sometimes, what seems easier and less costly really is more difficult and more expensive. For example, some people believe that drinking alcohol to deal with their problems is easier and less costly than it would be to work on their problems through therapy. However, is it really easier to get drunk every day and suffer social, economic, and health problems than it is to go to therapy? How much would one spend on alcohol over many years compared to the cost of going through therapy over a few months? Is it really harder to discuss one's problems (as unpleasant as that might be) with a therapist one-hour a week than it is to wake up with a hangover every morning, or deal with cirrhosis of the liver?

Realize that feeling miserable and behaving irrationally takes a lot of work! Getting what you want directly is usually much easier.

Attitude: "I have a right to feel (or think) the way I do..."

This attitude assumes that if we have a *right* to do something, it makes *sense* for us to do it. Obviously, this is not always the case. For example, a person has the right to call his or her boss a "jerk," but that does not mean that doing so would be rational!

People *do* have a right to feel, think, or do anything that they want, as long as they do not violate the rights of others. However, ask yourself, *"Is it in my best interest to feel or think the way I do? Is my thinking correct? Does my thinking and behavior help me to achieve my goals? Does my thinking and behavior help me feel the way that I want to feel?"*

As I mentioned earlier, cognitive-behavioral therapists/Rational Living Therapists do not tell people how they should feel. If a person wants to feel miserable, and justifies it with the notion that he or she has a right to feel that way, that is the person's business. Just keep in mind that the fact that a person has a right to feel miserable does not mean that it makes rational sense to do so.

Attitude: "It's easier said than done."

This is one of the most self-defeating, ridiculous statements I have ever heard! What *isn't* easier said than done? What most people really mean when they say this is that the task at hand will be (or may be) *too hard* for them to do. This perception of overwhelming difficulty quite naturally often leads them not even to attempt to achieve the goal.

Keep in mind that many people seeking psychotherapy have a history of *under*estimating their potential to achieve goals. Based on what you have reported and the experience of others similar to you, your therapist will assign tasks for you to complete that he or she believes you have the potential to achieve. Your therapist is *not* seeking to help you set yourself up for failure! So even if you have doubts about your potential, have at least some faith in your therapist's beliefs about you and take a chance to achieve your goals.

What appears to be "hard" to do often really is not—it's simply uncomfortable. I agree with Maultsby (1975) that the only time that it makes rational sense to think of behaviors as "hard" as opposed to "easy" is when we are discussing physical behaviors, not emotional or mental behaviors (feelings or thoughts). I'm sure that you would agree that it is harder (requires more energy, stamina, and effort) to carry a 100-pound bag of cement 50 feet than it is to carry a 50-pound bag the same distance. However, is it any harder, does it require any more effort, energy, or stamina to think, "I am smart" than to think, "I am dumb?" Of course not! What makes thinking, "I am smart" appear hard to think is that it feels *uncomfortable* to think that way. It's not hard, just uncomfortable.

Focusing on how you feel or behave as an indication of progress, rather than how you think.

Since most people seek therapy to feel and act better, it is very understandable that it would be their feelings and behaviors that they would use to gauge their progress in therapy. One problem with this approach to gauging progress is that sometimes people feel *worse* before they feel better (especially if in the past they had avoided thinking about their problems). Feeling worse could give a person the impression that he or she is *getting* worse, when in fact he or she is getting better.

Another problem with focusing on feelings and behaviors as an indication of progress in therapy is that if a person has ten misery-producing thoughts, rids herself of nine of them, but continues to think the one remaining thought every day, she will continue to feel miserable! If she were to focus only on how she feels as an indication of progress, she would think that she has not progressed at all, when in fact she is one thought away from consistent happiness!

Focus on your changes in thinking, and your feelings and behavior will follow.

Physical Factors

A person is in the best position to benefit from therapy when his or her body is functioning properly. A lack of sleep, poor eating, inactivity, and physical pain all contribute to decreased energy levels. These four factors are often symptoms of emotional problems, such as depression and anxiety.

Therefore, remedying these problems is important, especially if you find yourself being unable to work on your goals because of insufficient energy. While these symptoms often lessen and end as therapy progresses, sometimes medications or natural substances (vitamins, herbs) are necessary to "jump start" the patient (please refer to Chapter One).

If you are experiencing any of these problems, be certain to inform your therapist about your symptoms.

"Suffer From" Mentality

Unfortunately, some mental health professionals have "identified" and emphasized psychological "disorders" that actually do *not* exist as illnesses. For example, "Borderline Personality Disorder" does not exist as an *illness*. "Major Depression" does not exist as an illness. While they are listed as disorders in the *Diagnostic and Statistical Manual (DSM)*, they are not illnesses from which a person suffers, like the flu.

For example, when we look in the DSM and review the criteria for the diagnosis of "Borderline Personality Disorder," we see that the criteria are nothing more than behaviors, reactions, and attitudes. However, when we list them and apply the term "Borderline Personality Disorder" to them, now "it" is equated with a physical illness from which a person would suffer. The same is the case for "Major Depression" and most other diagnoses given by mental health professionals.

The problem with viewing yourself as "suffering" from depression, for example, is that it gives you the impression that there is this thing called "depression" that has invaded you (like the flu) causing you to be depressed. In fact, that is not the case.

I am not suggesting that people do not experience psychiatric symptoms that are the result of physical problems. Certainly they do. However, if an underactive thyroid causes a person's depressive symptoms, the person does not suffer from depression, he or she suffers from an underactive thyroid!

Most diagnostic labels in mental health are nothing more than a name for a group of behaviors—that's all! In the next chapter, you will learn that people do not "suffer from" depression, anxiety, anger, or problem behaviors. People *unintentionally* make themselves depressed, anxious, angry, and engage in problem behaviors. Thank goodness!

Expecting Instant Relief

I do not blame anyone for *wanting* instant relief! If there were something that I could do to help people feel relief instantly, I would do it! Most people seek treatment after they have suffered for a while and are tired of feeling the way they have been feeling. So they want relief as soon as possible. However, *expecting* instant relief is irrational. If we put therapeutic progress into perspective, cognitive-behavioral therapies help people help themselves "almost instantly" compared with other forms of therapy (the average number of sessions people spend in cognitive-behavioral therapy is sixteen, compared to years with psychoanalysis). However, it does take work and dedication to change how you feel. Completing therapeutic homework assignments will help speed your progress.

When people expect instant relief or believe they need it, they pressure themselves so much that they make it more difficult to feel better. Therefore, hope for relief as quickly as possible, but realize that you do not need relief quickly, you only want it. I do not blame you!

Poor Concentration

It is more difficult to learn something or to achieve a goal when we have a great deal of difficulty remaining focused. Poor concentration is often a symptom of emotional problems, especially depression and anxiety. Besides biochemical reasons why depression leads to concentration problems, the patient or client often comes to therapy with many issues to think about. Having many concerns in the forefront of one's attention interferes with one's ability to concentrate on what is going on around him or her. In other words, when your brain is clouded by upsetting thoughts, it is difficulty to pay attention to what you are trying to do.

Concentration problems usually lessen as people learn to resolve their problems rationally. However, if you have a concentration problem that is interfering with your ability to benefit from therapy, share your concern with your therapist.

Problematic Family Reactions

Many people seeking therapy have very supportive, loving families that encourage and assist them to feel and get better. Unfortunately, though, this is not always the case. Some clients' families actually discourage change. Sometimes families benefit from their loved-one's problem. For example, an insecure husband might try to sabotage any attempts that his wife makes to lose weight due to a concern that other men will think of his wife as attractive. So some families actually do have an interest in making certain that the patient does not get better.

Families attempt to sabotage progress in many ways. The most common sabotaging strategies include discouraging or interfering with homework completion, discouraging therapy session attendance, encouraging the client to think hopelessly, threatening harm, and attempting to create new problems.

If you believe that your family might be trying to sabotage your progress, avoid confronting them until you discuss your observations with your therapist.

Before moving on to the next chapter...

Answer the following questions:

–How good is it going to feel when you are feeling the way you want to feel?

–Who will be the first person to notice the positive changes in you?

–Who will be the most excited about your feeling better?

3

The Good News:
Our Emotional ABC's

Before learning *how* to feel better, it is important to learn what causes us to feel and act the way we do. After learning what causes our emotions and behaviors, you will know what needs to be changed to feel and do better.

A problem sometimes occurs when people have a very common incorrect idea of how our emotions work. Because of this incorrect assumption, they try to change the wrong thing. As a result, they continue to feel unwanted feelings, and they also feel frustrated because what they are doing to change their feelings is not working.

Image that I attempt to start my car, but the car will not start. I try it again, and the car still will not start. So I tell myself, "Aldo, I'll bet there is not enough air in the tires. That's why the car is not starting." So I get out my electric air pump and place some air in the tires. I attempt to start the car, and it continues not to start. So I then tell myself, "Maybe I didn't place enough air in the tires." If I continue down this path, I will have a car that does not start and that also has four flat tires. Obviously, the air pressure in the tires does not determine whether a car will start.

This is very similar to what happens when people have an incorrect idea of how our emotions work. As you will see, most people have an incorrect idea of what causes our feelings and behaviors!

Do not be surprised or alarmed if my explanation of how our emotions work feels a little strange or wrong to you. It is somewhat different from what people learn growing up. After you understand how our emotions actually work, you will be glad that what society teaches us about our emotions is wrong.

Good News #1: Our Emotional ABC's

Whenever a person with a healthy, normal brain experiences an emotional feeling or engages in a behavior, three things happen, and we call this the ABC's of Emotions.

(A) First we are **AWARE** of something (the "A" in the ABC's). In other words, we see something, hear something, or use our senses in some way to notice a situation, event, or condition.

(B) After we are aware of something our brain *automatically* begins to think or **BELIEVE** something about what we are aware of (the "B" in the ABC's). Also because of the way our brain works, we will think one of three different ways about this thing we are aware of—POSITIVELY, NEUTRALLY, or NEGATIVELY. An example of a positive thought is, "This is a good thing"; an example of a negative thought is, "This is a bad thing"; and an example of a neutral thought is "This isn't good or bad," or "It doesn't much matter to me."

(C) The way we think about what we are aware of then tells our brain how to make the rest of our body feel and tells our body how to act. We call this reaction the **EMOTIONAL CONSEQUENCE** (the "C" in the ABC's). A positive thought causes our body to feel a positive feeling (happy, excited), a negative thought causes a negative feeling (depression, anxiety, anger), and a neutral thought causes a neutral feeling.

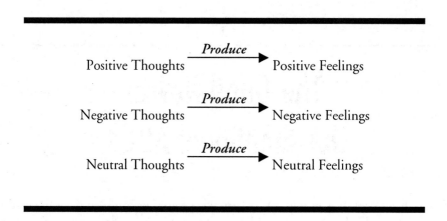

Most people do not know what a neutral feeling is because our society doesn't really teach this concept. The word "calm" best describes a neutral feeling. For example, have you ever sat in front of a television, not feeling particularly happy or upset so that you noticed, but just kind of sat there? If so, you were experiencing a neutral or calm emotion. However, if you were to approach most people who are calmly watching television and were to ask them, "What are you feeling right now?" it is likely they would tell you, "I'm not feeling anything." The only time we feel *nothing*, though, is if there is something wrong with our brain and body (like a severed spinal cord), if we are under general anesthesia (like for surgery), or if we are dead. Otherwise, what gets labeled as *no* feeling is usually *calm* or *neutral* feeling.

So, contrary to what most of us were taught growing up, it is what we *THINK* about what we are aware of that causes us to feel the way we feel and do what we do, *not* people, situations, things, or events!

Here is an example of the ABC's of Positive, Negative, and Neutral emotions.

ABC's of Emotions

As you can see in this example, the way a person *thinks* about the ending of a romantic relationship determines the way the person feels in reaction to it. Keep in mind, though, that this is the opposite of what society teaches us. How often have you said or heard other people say, "He upset me," "It made me mad," "She made me happy?" The reality, though, is that people, things, situations, and events *never* cause our emotional feelings and behaviors. ***What causes our feelings and behaviors is what we THINK about people, things, and situations.***

It makes sense for us to be very thankful that our emotions work the way I am describing to you. **If in fact people, situations, things, and events really did cause our emotional feelings, we would be their emotional slaves!** Any time someone wanted us to feel upset, we would *have to* feel upset because *they would be making us feel that way.* The faulty assumption that people cause our feelings and behaviors sometimes leads to people killing each other. They think to themselves, "This person is *making* me upset, and being upset is terrible. I've begged him, bribed him, pleaded with him, and threatened him to stop, but he won't. So the only way for me to feel better is to shoot him!"

What this good news also means is that a situation need not change for us to change the way we feel. To change the way we feel, we can change the way we think! In fact, even if an undesirable situation does improve, we will not feel better until we change our thinking along with it!

The fact that our thinking causes our feelings and behaviors is particularly important to keep in mind when we are confronted with situations over which we have very little or no control. Thinking thoughts that help us calmly accept a situation puts us in a better position to change it if possible.

Occasionally, someone will ask me, "Aren't there some things that are so bad that nearly everyone would feel upset…and if so, doesn't that mean that *the things* are causing you to be upset?" The answer to this question is, "No!" I recall a student once asking that same question. The rest of the class seemed to agree with her that there must be some things that are so bad that they cause people to be upset. So I asked her to give me an example. She said, "Nearly everyone would be upset if their house burned down, wouldn't they?" I agreed with her, nearly everyone would be upset under those circumstances. *However, that does not mean that the circumstances are what cause the upset!* I gave her and the class the following example:

Imagine there are three houses in a neighborhood located side-by-side. One house catches on fire, and as it burns, it ignites the other two houses. All three houses burn to the ground. The owner of the first house says, "This is more than I can handle…I'll never be able to recuperate from this…I might as well kill myself…" **As a result, Owner #1 feels very depressed.** The owner of the second house says, "Thank God! I've been trying to get out of this neighborhood for years, but no one would buy my lousy house…Now I can collect my insurance money and get the heck out of here!" **As a result, Owner #2 feels very happy.** The owner of the third house says, "My family and I really like this neighborhood, and it's going to be difficult to handle this situation…but it's important for me to calmly accept that this happened and deal with it rationally, because if I make myself miserable over it, I won't be able to do what's best for my family…" **As a result, Owner #3 feels calm or sad.**

In this example, it is clear that each homeowner's *thinking* about their house being destroyed is what caused their emotions. If it were an objective fact that the experience of one's home being destroyed *causes* emotional upset, ***all three homeowners would be upset!***

Keep in mind that we all have our own ideas about what is good, bad, and neutral. What would be the worst thing for one person could be an actual improvement for someone else. When I think of what would be one of the worst things in my life, I would say it would be losing my wife and children to death. Many people would agree with me. When people tell me that they believe that they will never be able to change the way they think to feel better because their situation is too bad, I think about a barber I once had. I'll call him "Fred the Barber." Fred had a busy barber shop in a small town in Southwestern Virginia. About four years before I met him, he suffered a loss in his life. His wife and three daughters were traveling home from his wife's parents' home when their car collided with a tractor trailer. In a very brief moment Fred's family was gone. imagine how he felt! Yet there he was, four years later, remarried, active in his church, and cutting my hair. He did not appear upset—to the contrary, he appeared to have an appreciation for life. I'm sure he continues to miss his wife and three daughters,

I don't like what is happening, but I need to focus on taking care of my family.

but he has moved on with his life. When people tell me they cannot accept personally unfortunate situations, I think about Fred and realize that the human brain allows us to accept anything that comes our way, no matter how very unfortunate it is to us.

Now that you know that your thoughts cause your feelings and behaviors, get in the habit of saying, "I upset myself…I made myself happy…My feelings are caused by my thoughts."

Good News #2: There are Three Ways of Feeling, Not Two

It also makes a great deal of sense for us to be very thankful that our bodies are capable of feeling three different types of emotions—positive, neutral, and negative. Our society teaches us that there are only two ways of feeling—either positively or negatively—good or bad. So something undesirable happens to you, like you lose your job. You say to yourself, "It doesn't make sense for me to feel **good** about this situation, so I must have to feel **bad**…" (Because there are only two choices, so we are told!). Thankfully, though, our bodies have always known what society hasn't—there are three ways of feeling. So you can have a ***neutral or calm*** reaction to an undesirable situation. That is precisely the goal of most cognitive therapy sessions—helping people move from feeling miserable to feeling along the lines of calm about a personally undesirable situation.

Feelings that are more along the lines of calm are "sad" as opposed to "depressed," "irritated," as opposed to "angry." The more along the lines of calm that we feel, the better we feel, and the better position we are in to do something to correct the undesirable situation.

Another important fact to keep in mind is that the opposite of feeling upset is *not* feeling happy. The opposite of feeling upset is *not* feeling upset, which is feeling calm. I point this out because sometimes if people seeking therapy do not understand this, they will ask their therapist, "Are you saying that I should be happy about my situation?" No! It would not make sense to be happy about something that you dislike! What we teach our clients is how to refuse to make themselves miserable over their undesirable situations—how to calmly accept them. It is very difficult, though, to be happy about anything as long as we are miserable about one thing! Calm acceptance of personally undesirable situations frees us up to be happy about other things.

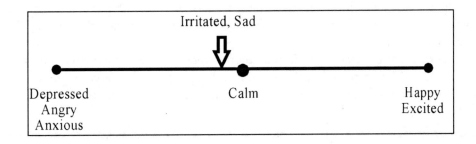

When we feel closer to "calm", we feel better,
and we are in a better position to handle most situations.

One common myth that many *professional therapists* believe of cognitive-behavioral therapy is that it teaches people not to feel feelings. If these therapists understood brain functioning, they would realize that a person *always* feels feelings, unless he or she is under anesthesia or if there is something wrong with his or her brain. Cognitive-behavioral therapy doesn't teach people *not* to feel, rather, it teaches them how to *more calmly* react to situations over which they are currently upset.

Another common myth about calm feelings is that if a person reacts calmly to something, that means that he or she does not care about it. Nonsense! Calmly accepting something only means that you refuse to make yourself miserable over it. It does not mean that you do not want to do something about it!

Yet another myth is that cognitive-behavioral therapists teach people that they are not permitted to feel emotional upset. More nonsense! People have the right to feel and behave any way they choose, as long as their behaviors do not violate the rights of others. We teach people how to feel the way they want to feel without judging their emotional preferences.

Now that you understand that your thoughts cause your feelings and behaviors, I'm sure that you realize the importance of paying attention to your thoughts in those situations with which you are currently struggling. As a result, your therapist will ask you to complete the ABC Worksheets at the end of this chapter. If you happen to upset yourself or behave in a way that is counterproductive, break your reaction or behavior down into the ABC's of Emotions.

Reflexive Thoughts: Why Sometimes it Seems as Though "Things" Cause Our Feelings

Sometimes when people are completing their emotional ABC's, they will realize what they were aware of (A), and they will know how they felt and what they did (C), but they will not know what they thought (B) about it. They will say, "It happened so quickly, I don't know what I was thinking about it." When this is the case, it is likely that a **Reflexive (or "Reflex") Thought** was triggered.

A reflexive thought is a thought that is so well-learned that it no longer needs to be thought consciously—it is stored in the brain, ready for action. The second something reminds your brain of a reflexive thought, it is triggered, and you then feel the feeling that is consistent with that thought. In fact, it only takes 1/10,000th of a second for an impulse to travel through your brain. That's how quickly a person can react to something.

For example, pretend that as you are driving a little too closely behind the car in front of you, you suddenly see the car's break lights illuminate. What would you do? Naturally, you would instantly apply your breaks to stop your car. However, before applying your breaks, would you need to say to yourself, "Gee, I see that this car in front of me is stopping suddenly, so I'd better put my foot on the break?" Of course not! You would almost *instantly* apply your breaks and later marvel at how quickly you reacted. What would allow you to apply your breaks quickly is a well-learned reflexive thought about what it takes to stop a car. That reflexive thought is something like, "For me to stop a car, I need to put my foot on the break pedal." How did that thought become so well-learned? I'm sure that when you were a child, you saw adults placing their foot on the break pedal to stop the car. When you were old enough to drive, you began practicing the brake-applying belief each time that you put your foot on the break pedal. Consequently, the belief has become so well-learned that it is stored in the brain, ready for action. The instant the reflexive thought is triggered, the foot goes on the break pedal.

These almost instant reactions give people the impression that they did not think anything. It often also gives them the impression that "A" caused "C." Remember, though, that a thought precedes everything that we do (except simple reflexes, like a leg jerking when the knee is tapped).Remember that the ABC's of Emotions are:

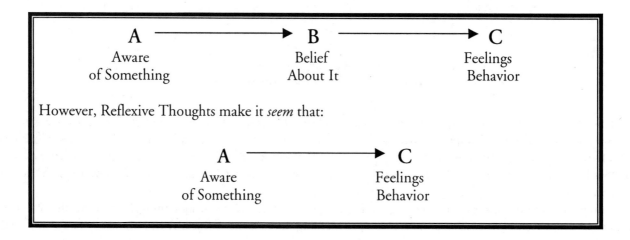

Reflexive thoughts are very helpful to us when they help us protect our life and health. Reflexive thoughts can be a problem when they are well-learned **irrational** beliefs. For example, let's say I have a reflexive thought that, "People must treat me with respect and kindness, and if they don't, it is terrible, awful, and I need to be really upset about it…" Let's also say that I began thinking this way at a very young age. After thinking this way for several years, the thought becomes a reflexive thought. This reflexive thought is so well-learned that it is stored in my brain ready for action. So I go to my favorite department store, do my shopping, and take my items to the checkout line. The clerk says to me, "Aldo, that is the ugliest tie I have ever seen!" I then *instantly* upset myself, and it would seem that "A" caused "C."

Actually, there is a thought that was triggered to create the anger—"People must treat me with respect and kindness, and if they don't, it is terrible, awful, and I need to be really upset about it..." This thought would have traveled through my brain so quickly (since it is so well-learned) that I would not even realize I thought it!

Remember, though, that we must identify our thoughts to be able to change them. But in a situation like this, it appears that we haven't thought anything. Maxie C. Maultsby, Jr., M.D. suggests asking the following question to uncover reflexive thoughts:

"I'm *acting* as if I believe what about this situation?"

Reflex Thoughts

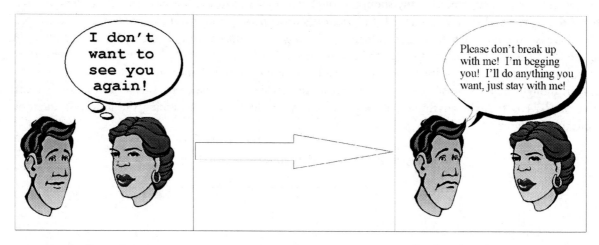

A. Awareness   C. Emotional Consequence

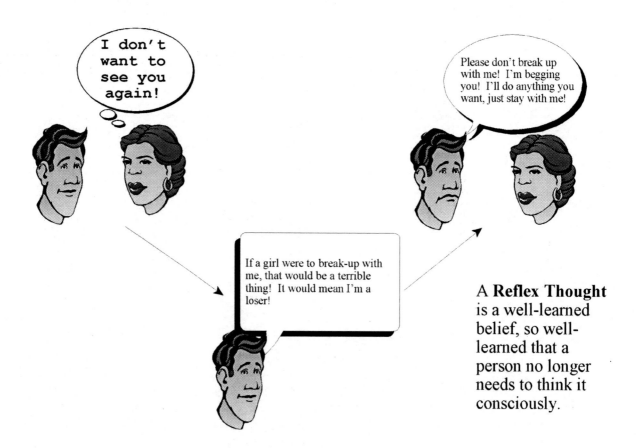

A **Reflex Thought** is a well-learned belief, so well-learned that a person no longer needs to think it consciously.

In this example, I know that I *could not* have thought, "What a wonderful thing it is to have my tie called ugly. I hope that she says it again!" and felt angry at the same time. Since I felt angry, I acted as if I believed that I didn't like what she said to me. Then I might ask myself, "What didn't I like about it?" I probably would come to the conclusion that I thought it was terrible that she had not treated me in a kind manner.

Unless there is something seriously wrong with your brain, your thoughts will make sense for the way you feel. How you feel and act will be a reflection of what you are thinking. The more you learn about the different beliefs that cause the different emotions, the better you will be at uncovering reflexive thoughts. Chapter Seven discusses the common mental mistakes associated with problematic emotional reactions.

Incomplete Thoughts

After teaching you the ABC's of Emotions, your therapist will likely ask you to break your unwanted emotional reactions down into the ABC's. When doing so, a common mistake people make is to omit the actual belief that causes the emotion. For example:

A (What you are aware of)	**B** (What you thought about it)	**C** (How You Felt)
My husband came home at 4:00 in the morning.	He's having an affair.	Angry Anxious

To say, "He's having an affair" isn't enough because that does not tell us *what you think about the idea that he's having an affair.* Unless we assume what one thinks about the possibility that a husband is having an affair, we could only guess what the reaction would be at "C"—how she felt and acted. To demonstrate:

A (What you are aware of)	**B** (What you thought about it)	**C** (How You Felt)
My husband came home at 4:00 in the morning.	He's having an affair, **and the rotten S.O.B. shouldn't treat me this way after I gave him the best years of my life. Now what will I do? I'm going to be alone, and that will be terrible!**	Angry Anxious
My husband came home at 4:00 in the morning.	He's having an affair, **and That's wonderful, because now I can divorce him and really cash in!**	Happy
My husband came home at 4:00 in the morning.	He's having an affair, **but it really doesn't matter because I'm divorcing him anyway.**	Calm

As you can see, the underlying belief determines the emotional reaction experienced. Therefore, as you break down your emotional reactions into the ABC's, make certain that you complete your thoughts.

Identify Your Thoughts

So the goal is to discover what you are thinking whenever you upset yourself or engage in behaviors that you wish to eliminate. Your therapist will then teach you how to determine whether your thinking is rational or irrational. If your thinking *is* rational, you will want to keep it because it is helping you. However, when people experience significant, unwanted emotions or engage in problematic behaviors, they are usually mistaken in their thinking for one reason or another. If your thinking is irrational, you will want to eliminate it and replace it with rational thoughts. Your therapist will teach you how to do that.

People often ask me, "Is it possible for a person to change the way he or she thinks? If so, how can a person learn how to think differently?" Actually, not only is it possible for us to "change" our thoughts, we do it virtually every day. For most thoughts we think on a daily basis, we do not have to "learn" how to change them. If I were to place money into a soda pop machine, I would be acting as if I believed, "This machine is going to give me a can of soda pop." However, should the machine be broken and not give me the pop, I would very quickly and easily change my mind about this machine. One reason I could very quickly change my thinking about the machine is that the facts about the machine would be right before me. I would have seen that the machine hadn't given me the pop.

However, well-learned, important thoughts often take a little more work to change. Keep in mind that we do not waste our time thinking thoughts we know are not correct. But just because we believe something to be true does not mean it is a fact. Cognitive-behavioral therapy helps people to determine for themselves whether their thoughts are worth thinking. It then teaches them how to replace old, problematic thoughts with new, healthier thoughts.

We learn thoughts the same way we learn how to type, drive, read, etc.… It is the same process. What makes a new way of thinking a habit for us is practice. Cognitive-behavioral therapy teaches people several effective methods to practice new thoughts and behaviors. It really is not hard at all. It just takes practice.

A New Habit to Develop

Rather than saying, "He upset me…, she made me mad…, it made me nervous…," get in the habit of saying, "I upset myself…I make myself happy…I create all of my emotions by the way I think…"

Some people make the good-sounding, but problematic statement, "I let someone upset me." To say that we let people upset us is to imply that they have the power to upset us, and we have allowed them to do so. As you have learned, though, people *do not* have the power to upset us. They say and do things, and *our thinking about what they say or do* then upsets us. Therefore, rather than saying, "I let him upset me," say, "I upset myself over what he said."

An Important Note

People often confuse the idea of "upsetting oneself" with "choosing to upset oneself." Cognitive-behavioral therapists teach that our thoughts cause our emotions and behaviors. This is not to say that we are always happy with the way we think, or that we are simply choosing to feel miserable because we have nothing better to do! People unintentionally make themselves miserable or act in otherwise problematic ways.

People, even when they understand and practice rational self-counseling, sometimes upset themselves because they do not know any other way to think about the situation at hand. They direct themselves to feel upset, but they would not do this if they knew another way to think. That's what this book is all about—learning how to think rationally consistently, which, in turn, makes you feel and act rationally.

ABC Situations

<u>A</u> (What I was Aware Of)	<u>B</u> (What I thought about A)	<u>C</u> (How I Felt / What I did)

ABC Situations

<u>A</u> (What I was Aware Of)	<u>B</u> (What I thought about A)	<u>C</u> (How I Felt / What I did)

4

Thoughts and Underlying Assumptions

In Rational Living Therapy, we make the distinction between **thoughts** and **underlying assumptions**.

Underlying assumptions are beliefs that are usually pervasive, which means that they affect more than one area of a person's life. The more basic the underlying assumption, the more areas of one's life it will affect.

For example, an underlying assumption, "My husband doesn't love me," would affect a woman's relationship with her husband. A more basic underlying assumption, like, "People do not love me," would affect many relationships, not just with her husband.

We have underlying assumptions about ourselves and the world around us. For example, when people drive down a two-lane road, they do so with the assumption, "I'm going to remain in my lane, and the people coming toward me are going to remain in their lane." If people did not assume this, they would either never drive on a two-lane road, or there would be chaos when they did.

Underlying assumptions primarily are **non-conscious**, which means that when a person asks you, "What do you think about that?" it is not likely that you will express an underlying assumption. What you likely are to state is a **thought**.

A **thought** is specific to a situation. It is an interpretation of a situation. It is how you "see" it, and the reason for this interpretation often is that an underlying assumption feeds the interpretation. For example, let's say that a wife has the following underlying assumption about her husband:

He doesn't love me!

So it's Valentine's Day. On the way home from work, her husband buys her a dozen roses, gives them to her, and says, "Happy Valentine's Day, Dear!" During their next marital therapy session, he tells the therapist, "You know doc, I just can't figure her out. It was Valentine's Day, so I bought her some roses and gave them to her, and she told me to shove them." What might she have **thought** about the fact that he gave her the roses since she has an **underlying assumption** that he does not love her? Possible thoughts include:

He must want something from me.

He must be feeling guilty about something.

He only bought me those flowers because he had to.

The day after Valentine's Day, he does something to help her in some way, and her thoughts again are something like:

He must want something from me.

He must be feeling guilty about something.

He only helped me because he had to.

Each time he does something "nice" for her, her immediate interpretation or thought would be something along this line of thinking.

Now let's say that she has an even more basic underlying assumption, like, "I am not loveable. There is something wrong with me. So I'm sure *people* wouldn't like me if they really knew me." I am certain that you can see how many areas of her life that underlying assumption would affect. Not only is this why she assumes that her *husband* does not love her, but this is why she tends to avoid *other people* as well.

Let's look at how this appears if we diagram it.

Why We Focus on Underlying Assumptions in Rational Living Therapy

The above example illustrates how sometimes it appears to us that we have more problems than we actually do. If we were to ask her how many problems she wants to discuss, it is likely that she would say "three." However, if the underlying assumption, "He doesn't love me" is incorrect, then she actually has one problem (the mistaken assumption) that gives her the impression that she has three.

Focusing on underlying assumptions **speeds the progress of therapy**. By focusing on underlying assumptions, your therapist can help you dealing with several problems with one effort by working on a common thread that might be causing the problems.

Focusing on underlying assumptions also **helps to produce long-term results** because it is addressing and correcting the *cause* of the symptoms, not just the symptoms themselves. For example, a person walks past a group of people and they begin laughing. Most people in that situation assume that they are being laughed at. Good (but incomplete) therapy sounds like this:

Therapist: "Was there anything about you that they mentioned that would give us any indication that they were laughing at you? Did you hear them mention your name, or something that you were wearing, or anything like that?"

Client: "No, they just laughed."

Therapist: "So it very well could be that it was a coincidence, that they were not laughing at you at all. There is no point in assuming that they were laughing at you, so you might as well just forget about it."

This looks like good therapy, but it is incomplete therapy. I would wonder why the person was still upset about it a week later to discuss it with me. I would take it a step further with the client.

Me: "Let's pretend for a moment that in fact they were laughing at you. As far as you are concerned, why would that be a bad thing?"

Client: "Because I hate being laughed at. I can't stand it."

Me: "While it is very common for people to think that they are being laughed at in these situations, is there any particular reason why you assumed that they were laughing at you? Do you think there is a reason for people to laugh at you?"

Client: "Well, I've always thought of myself as being too short and kind of unattractive."

If a therapist only focused on helping the client refuse to "jump to conclusions," it is likely that the client would continue to have problems in similar situations due to two problematic underlying assumptions:

"To be laughed at is a terrible thing that I cannot stand"; and
"I'm too short and unattractive."

To help the client obtain long-term results, it would be important to help him correct these two problematic underlying assumptions. Without doing so, they would lie dormant, waiting to be activated by situations, like walking past a group of people that starts laughing.

Your therapist, at times, will ask you questions, like:

For you, why would that be bad?

If that were the case, what would that mean?

When he or she asks these questions, it is to help uncover these underlying thoughts.

5

About Problems

Rational Living Therapists agree with Dr. Albert Ellis (1988), the originator of Rational Emotive Behavior Therapy, that "problems" can be categorized into two types—practical and emotional.

Practical problems are situations and circumstances that make it difficult for us to achieve our goals. For example, if your car were to break down on the way to work, the car being broken would be a practical problem because it would make it difficult to achieve your goal of getting to work, which would make it difficult to earn money that day, which would make it more difficult to pay your bills.

Emotional problems are usually reactions to practical problems. An emotional problem is the unwanted "upset" that you feel when upsetting yourself over practical problems. In the above example, if you felt angrier than you wanted, your anger would be considered an emotional problem. (Please keep in mind, though, that the term "emotional problem" in this sense does not imply abnormality.)

If your car were to break down on the way to work, and you felt miserable in reaction to it, it is likely that you would view yourself as having one problem—your broken car. In fact, though, you would actually have two problems—your car (a practical problem) and your misery (an emotional problem)!

Would you agree with me that humans like to have the fewest number of problems possible at any given time? Certainly! Now, if you had your choice between having your car broken and feeling miserable, or having your car broken and feeling calm, which would you pick? Also consider this fact—*the car does not care how you emotionally react to it!* The car will be just as broken whether you are happy, calm, or miserable in reaction to it. Therefore, if there is no requirement that you make yourself miserable in reaction to the car being broken, why not learn how to react more calmly to it, and cut your problems in half?

This is the essence of what is known as **stoicism**—that reality does not care how we emotionally react to it. Since reality does not care, we might as well learn how to react calmly to our personally undesirable situations! This realization itself has helped many people effectively deal with personally difficult and challenging situations and daily living disappointments. Therefore, an excellent rational self-statement that can be applied to any situation is:

> **"I'm going to have my problem whether I'm miserable or not,**
> **so I might as well give up the misery!"**

Actually, there *is* a third type of problem—**imagined**. Sometimes we think that we have a practical problem when in fact we do not. Or we might be mistaken in terms of to what extent our situation is problematic. We might think that our car is broken when in fact it is not. Or we might think that the cause of it not working properly is more serious and complicated than it actually is.

No matter the circumstances, you can find a rational way to feel better!

That's a pretty bold, but accurate statement. Why? Because when people make themselves miserable or act in personally problematic ways, they make one of two correctable mistakes. Either they:

(1) are mistaken about the facts of their circumstances, so that they are upset about something that isn't, or are reacting to something that isn't, or

(2) they are correct about their circumstances. Their situation really is the way that they think it is, but they think that being upset is either necessary, important, unavoidable, or that there would be something wrong with them if they were to react differently. Often, though, it is simply a matter of a person not knowing how to react any other way.

Being mistaken about the facts of one's circumstances is problematic because it leads a person to act in way that is not appropriate for his or her situation. For example, a person might notice a lump on his arm and think that the lump is a cancerous tumor when in fact it is a harmless cyst. If he thinks that it is cancer and that he is doomed to die as a result, he might decide (irrationally) to commit suicide, rather than face a slow, painful death. Hopefully, someone would help him to realize that the lump is only a harmless cyst.

What if the lump really is a cancerous tumor? Now what? This is when cognitive-behavioral therapy is particularly helpful in that it teaches people how to more calmly accept their current reality. I used cancer as an example because most people react with complete horror at the thought that they or a loved one might have it. Why? Because most people believe that horror is either necessary, important, or unavoidable. Most often, people simply do not know that a concerned, calm reaction is possible. Cognitive-behavioral therapy teaches people that responding to personally undesirable situations calmly is possible and helpful.

The rest of this book will show you how to correct both mistakes

6

The Three Rational Questions

Now that you know that our thinking causes our feelings and behaviors, you know that it is important to take a good, critical look at the thoughts that lead to our *unwanted* feelings and behaviors. We want to keep our good, *rational* thoughts because these thoughts help us to feel good and to do well. Conversely, we want to get rid of *irrational* thoughts because they make us feel bad and perform not so well.

How do we distinguish between a **rational thought** and an **irrational thought**? One way is to apply the **Three Rational Questions** to our thoughts. These Three Rational Questions are an adaptation of Dr. Maxie C. Maultsby's "Five Criteria for Rational Thinking."

The Three Rational Questions

1. Is my thinking based on fact?

2. Does my thinking help me achieve my goals?

3. Does my thinking help me feel the way I want to feel?

Three "yes" answers means the thought is rational.

Dr. Maultsby was the first cognitive-behavioral theorist to develop criteria for rational behavior. His questions remain a major contribution to the field, as they have enabled people to objectively identify problem thoughts on their own. While I have narrowed the "rational questions" to three, Maultsby's other two questions, "Does my behavior help me protect my life and health?" and "Does my behavior help me avoid unwanted conflict with others?" are clinically useful. For a complete description of the Five Rules of Rational Thinking, read "Coping Better, Any Time, Any Where" by Maxie C. Maultsby, Jr., M.D.

Let us now look at each of the Three Rational Questions in detail.

Rational Question #1: "Is my thinking based on fact?"

This question asks, "Is what I'm thinking the way things really are?" Most people assume that their thinking is based on fact, or they would not waste their time acting on it. Keep in mind, though, that when we talk to ourselves, there are three kinds of statements we make—

Jokes, Lies, and Sincere Statements.

We do not act on jokes—when we *know* that we are just kidding when we say something. We do not act on lies—when we *know* that what we are saying is not accurate. We only act on sincere statements. The problem is, though, that what we sincerely believe to be true is not necessarily based on fact. But the human brain does not care whether what we think is *accurate*. It only cares whether we *sincerely believe it*. When we sincerely believe something, our brain tells our body how to react accordingly.

A good example of this is what people in Europe thought at one time. They would look out at the ocean, and it looked like it ended at the horizon. As a result, they concluded that the world was flat—that if a person were to sail beyond a certain point, he would drop off the Earth. Because they sincerely believed that the world was flat, they would not sail past a certain point, and thought that anyone who would attempt to do so was not well.

However, one guy, Christopher Columbus, proved that what they had sincerely believed to be true was not based on fact. He sincerely believed that the world was round. Because of his belief, he was willing to sail beyond where others were willing to sail, until he discovered the new world.

Since most people naturally will be inclined to answer this question, "yes, of course my thinking is based on fact," we had better have good techniques to help us be more objective about our thinking.

THE CAMERA CHECK OF PERCEPTIONS

One technique to help determine whether our thinking is based on fact is the **Camera Check of Perceptions** (Maultsby, 1984). When utilizing this technique, ask yourself, "If I were to take a picture of the situation I'm describing to myself, or if I were to use a video camera to record it and played the tape back, would it show what I am saying about the situation?"

Keep in mind that the human brain and a camera work alike in that both take in information and produce a visual image. However, a camera will *only* take a picture of what is in front of it. A camera does not add anything to the picture, take anything away, or distort the image unless there is something wrong with it or it (nowadays) is designed to do so. The human brain, on the other hand, does not have that limitation. The human brain can add to, subtract from, and otherwise distort the image based on what we already think or believe about what we are seeing.

As a practical example, someone might ask me, "Was Suzie at the party the other night?" If I know that Suzie *usually* goes to parties, I might think for a minute (trying to visualize the party), and say, "Yes, I believe she was." In fact, though, she wasn't there, but I inadvertently placed her in my mental picture of the party.

When our description of a situation is not what a camera would show, our description is not accurate. When our description is not accurate, our reaction is inappropriate for the situation.

Let's say a person is feeling somewhat depressed because he is thinking, "My wife always yells at me. She is always yelling at me." Utilizing the camera check of perceptions, I would ask him:

<u>Me</u>: "If we had video cameras positioned throughout your home recording the events of this past week, and now you and I were to sit down and watch this tape, would it show your wife *always* yelling at you? I hope not, because what does the word *always* mean?"

<u>Client</u>: "Well, I guess *always* means constantly, twenty-four hours a day, seven days a week."

<u>Me</u>: "That's right. Now, is that what a camera would show?"

<u>Client</u>: "No, it sure wouldn't."

<u>Me</u>: "Good. What would a camera actually show?"

<u>Client</u>: "It would show her yelling at me Tuesday, and, uh, Friday."

<u>Me</u>: "Obviously, there is a difference in how you feel when you say, "My wife always yells at me," as opposed to, "My wife *sometimes* yells at me, certainly more than I wish she would.""

The camera check of perceptions not only helps us make certain that we have our facts straight, but it also helps us make certain that we say what we mean and mean what we say to ourselves.

Sometimes people will say, "That isn't what I *meant* when I said that my wife always yells at me, that she yells at me twenty-four hours a day, seven days a week." However, the human brain does not care what we mean—it cares what we say. For example, imagine as you are driving down the road a police officer pulls you over and tells you that you were traveling ten miles per hour over the speed limit. He then tells you, "I'm going to have to give you a ticket for $1,000." You say, "One-thousand dollars, that's outrageous. Why so much?" The officer responds by saying, "Oh, I'm sorry. Did I say $1,000? I meant $10." To you, until he corrected himself, would it have mattered what he said or what he meant? Obviously, what mattered is what he *said*. The same is the case when we talk to ourselves.

To think accurately, our verbal thoughts must be accurate. Our verbal thoughts are composed of sentences, and each sentence is made up of words. Each word in a sentence is important as is described in...

A Quick Psychology Lesson

The late Russian research physiologist, Ivan Pavlov, studied the digestive system of dogs by conducting experiments. He had machines that collect gastric juices connected to their stomachs. As most people who have owned a dog know, dogs salivate at the sight of food. Dogs do not need to learn to salivate at the sight of food. They are born that way. However, Pavlov accidentally discovered that the dogs began salivating to other stimuli associated with their receiving food, i.e., the sound of him getting the food. Through experiments, he discovered what is known as **classical conditioning**, that is, that when something that *does* presently produce a response is paired enough times with something that *doesn't*, eventually the thing that didn't produce the response does. For example:

Food -------------------- **Salivation**

(Food triggers salivation.)

Bell + Food -------------------- **Salivation**

(Bell is sounded right before presenting food.)

Bell -------------------- **Salivation**

(After a while, the bell alone triggers salivation.)

The continual pairing of the bell and the food led the dogs to salivate *to the bell alone* after a while.

As Maxie C. Maultsby, Jr., M.D. has noted, *"Words are to humans as the bell was to Pavlov's dog."* Words are conditioned to having meaning, and we begin being conditioned to the meaning of words very early in life. The words that we use when we think produce conditioned emotions in us. Therefore, it is very important that we think and speak to ourselves accurately—that we say what we mean, and mean what we say.

To demonstrate that words are conditioned, take my mother as an example. My mother was born and raised in Italy and moved to the United States when she was twenty-one-years-old. Although she has been in the US for many years, she continues to report that "Italian swear words" seem worse than "American swear words" to her, though they essentially have the same meaning. She was conditioned as a child to believe that the Italian swear words were very bad and should never be spoken. She didn't receive quite the same threatening message about the American words; thus, her reaction to them is less negative, though they are equivalent in meaning to their Italian counterparts.

So when it comes to our emotions, the words we say to ourselves are ***all important***.

Obviously the camera check of perceptions can be helpful in assisting us to say what we mean and mean what we say. As an example, one of my first clients years ago said to me, "My husband is a dirty rat!" She then went on to describe the things he did that she did not like. After we talked for a while, the following occurred:

<u>Me</u>: "O.K. Do you remember last week we talked about the Rational Questions?"

<u>Client</u>: "Yes I do."

<u>Me</u>: "Good. As you might recall, the first rational question is, "Is my thinking based on fact?" Now, if I were to take a picture of your husband and take it downstairs to the secretary, what would she see in the picture?"

<u>Client</u>: "She'd see my husband."

<u>Me</u>: "Okay. Let's pretend she doesn't know your husband. What would she see in the picture?"

<u>Client</u>: "She'd see a man."

<u>Me</u>: "Right. And if I were to show the picture to the rest of the therapists in the office, what would they see in the picture?"

<u>Client</u>: "A man."

<u>Me</u>: "Right. Now what did you call your husband a few minutes ago?"

<u>Client</u>: "Oh yea. I called him a dirty rat, but that's just an expression!"

<u>Me</u>: "Not really. You see, I know you are not psychotic and do not actually see him as being a dirty, furry little rodent. But when you call him a dirty rat, you feel just as bad as you would if in fact he were a dirty rat. Tell me, what do you think of dirty rats?"

<u>Client</u>: "They are disgusting!"

<u>Me</u>: "So you see you probably have thought they were disgusting for a long time, so that the mere mention of the words "dirty rat" conjures up disgusting feelings, right?"

<u>Client</u>: "Exactly!"

<u>Me</u>: "So as if your upset over what he does to you weren't bad enough, you unintentionally make matters worse for yourself simply by calling him, to yourself, a dirty rat."

<u>Client</u>: "I see!"

<u>Me</u>: "Now tell me…Is your husband "a man who does things you do not like" or a "dirty rat?"

<u>Client</u>: "He is a man who does things I don't like."

<u>Me</u>: "And which way of thinking makes you feel better?"

<u>Client</u>: "That he is a man who does things I don't like."

<u>Me</u>: "Right. Now that doesn't take away from what he actually does to you, but having a more accurate description of him makes you feel better. It also helps you to act differently toward him, which might encourage him to treat you differently."

Do your best, therefore, to say what you mean and mean what you say to yourself.

The Common Mental Mistakes

Another fact-finding approach is to determine if you are making one of the common mental mistakes people make. These mental mistakes are described in detail in the next chapter. After reading the next chapter, you will learn how committing these mistakes makes your thinking inconsistent with fact.

Therefore, I strongly encourage you to act like a detective with your thinking. You do not need to examine all of your thinking, just thinking related to areas or things about which you are concerned. In those situations, refuse to take for granted that your thinking is accurate. To do so, ask yourself:

–Do I have proof that my thinking is correct?

–Do I have proof that my thinking is incorrect?

–What are other possible explanations?

–What is the evidence?

Sometimes you will not know if your thought is based on fact or not without some investigation. You might need to turn to someone who is knowledgeable about the circumstances with which you are concerned. For example, a person develops a lump on his arm. His immediate thought is, "This must be cancer." At this point, does he know he has cancer? No. On the other hand, does he know it is not cancer? No. It is important for him to acknowledge that he does not know either way and to get the lump examined by a physician.

More Help with Rational Question #1

Have you ever hoped that something that you thought was incorrect? Sometimes we hope and pray that what we are thinking is incorrect! On the next page, write down any thoughts that have been troubling you that you hope are incorrect. At this point, I am not encouraging you *actually to believe* that they are incorrect, but only to acknowledge that there could be advantages to being wrong!

Thoughts that I Hope are Incorrect!

<u>Distressing Thought</u>

<u>Why do I hope it is Incorrect?</u>

Example: *"No girl would ever want to go out with me."*

If I'm wrong, I'll end up with a girlfriend!

Example: *"I'm a nothing and a nobody."*

If I'm wrong, I'll feel much better!

Rational Question #2: "Does my thinking help me achieve my goals?"

Any thought that does not help you achieve your goals or is contrary to them would not pass the second rational question. The belief, "I know I'm not going to pass the test tomorrow, so I'm not going to study," certainly would not help a person achieve his or her goal of passing the test. Therefore, this thought would not pass the second rational question.

Sometimes a thought *indirectly* interferes with achieving a goal. Imagine that while a college student is studying one evening for an exam to be taken the following day, her boyfriend telephones and tells her that he cannot keep his date with her that they had planned for the weekend. "Darn him, he should not treat me this way," she exclaims. Because of her belief and resultant upset, she decides to quit studying for the exam. Her performance on the test the next day is not as good as she had hoped it would be. While her belief about her boyfriend's behavior had nothing to do with the test, the upsetting thoughts did, nevertheless, affect her performance on it.

Rational Question #3: "Does my thinking help me feel the way I want to feel?"

If you are feeling an emotion you do not want to feel, the thinking that is causing those feelings would not pass the third rational question. Keep in mind, however, that this rational question encourages us to feel the way we want to feel, *without*, alcohol, drugs, or engaging in otherwise dangerous behavior.

So, What *is* Rational?

For a thought to be considered **RATIONAL**, it must pass all three rational questions (for a total of three "yes" answers). If your thought is rational, you want to hold onto it because it serves you well. If you answer "no" to one or more of the three questions, your thought is an **IRRATIONAL THOUGHT**. If your thought is irrational, you will want to learn how to refuse to think it any longer, develop a new, rational thought to replace it, and practice this new thought until it feels comfortable to you and becomes your way of thinking. You will learn how to do this in the following chapters.

As you can see, rational thinking is not necessarily positive thinking. Simple "positive thinking" is thinking that *does not* necessarily consider facts, but is thought simply to feel better. For example, if we had planned an outdoor activity for several months and the day before the activity the weather forecasters predict an eighty-percent chance of rain, we might upset ourselves over that fact. "Positive thinking" would be, "I know the forecasters are calling for rain, but I'll just choose to believe that it won't." Rational thinking would be, "As much as I hope it won't rain tomorrow, it looks like it's going to…If it does, I'll be disappointed, but I'll refuse to make myself miserable over it…It would be a good idea to make alternate plans in case it does rain…"

A Special Note

Ideally, any self-help method would be most beneficial if it could be implemented *during* a personally difficult event. Rational self-counseling can be implemented in such a manner with practice. Your diligent practice of the techniques and concepts presented in this book will do the following for you:

(1) Enable you to analyze your upset over a situation rationally after it has happened, thus helping you determine effective measures for avoiding future upset over similar situations;

(2) Enable you to counsel yourself rationally during personally difficult situations to minimize upset;

(3) Enable you to prevent upset by rationally predicting problems and appropriately preparing yourself.

No matter how well you know the techniques described in this book, you will encounter new situations in your life with which you have not rationally dealt, and, consequently, you will upset yourself. However, you are learning skills to avoid repeatedly upsetting yourself over the same and similar issues.

As you continue to break down your unwanted emotions and behaviors into the ABC's, begin applying the Rational Questions to the thoughts related to those situations. Share your experience with applying the Rational Questions with your therapist.

Now that you know the Three Rational Questions, the next chapter discusses the common mistakes people make in their thinking. Remember, understanding the common mental mistakes will help you to more accurately determine whether your thinking is based on fact.

7

The Common Mental Mistakes

"Much of What is Considered Common Sense is Actually Nonsense"

The human brain is a fascinating organ capable of much more than we may ever know. The brain plays a very active role in controlling the organs of the body. It monitors and controls nearly all of the body's activities. Your brain gets concerned when your temperature is too high or too low. It gets concerned when you haven't had enough sleep or enough to eat. And your brain attempts to regulate your temperature, appetite, and sleep accordingly.

However, the human brain *is very passive* when it comes to your emotional feelings. Your brain does not care what you think. It does not care if you think a rational thought or an irrational thought. Furthermore, the brain doesn't have a built-in mechanism that makes us think only good, rational thoughts. The brain does not have a built-in nonsense filter that filters out mistaken, irrational thoughts. I wish it did! However, your healthy brain will make your body feel the way it should feel based on how you are thinking.

We do not sincerely hold a belief that we believe is incorrect. This is why we do not often stop to evaluate our thoughts for their accuracy. **So your doubts, worries, fears, shoulds, musts, and have-to's have gotten a free ride for a long time! They have, for the most part, gone unchallenged...completely free to make you miserable!** *Now it is time to refuse to give these potentially problematic thoughts a free ride and, instead, learn how to dispute them rationally!*

One goal of cognitive-behavioral therapy is to (in effect) build a nonsense filter in your brain. With this imaginary filter, you will be able to detect problematic thoughts and, therefore, avoid thinking them. You will build the nonsense filter by learning the common mental mistakes listed below.

You do not have to memorize the name of each mistake. The important thing is to understand the concept of the mistakes and have them understood well enough to be able to recognize if you are thinking in those terms. It's likely that you will begin noticing others making these mistakes as well!

The Common Mental Mistakes

A variation of the first ten mental mistakes was first described by Dr. Aaron Beck (1976) and later by Dr. David Burns (1980). I have expanded this list to twenty-six.

(1) All-or-None Thinking

People unintentionally cheat themselves out of a great deal of happiness when they think in all-or-none terms. All-or-none thinking is the mistake of viewing things in black-or-white, everything-or-nothing terms. It is viewing things as only one way or another. When a light is connected to a conventional "on/off" switch, the light is either on or off. Most things in life have a middle ground, like a light connected to a dimmer switch. There are degrees to which the light is on.

Few aspects of our lives have no middle ground. Examples of all-or-none thinking include:

"A person is either *ugly* or *good looking*..."

"A person is either *dumb* or *intelligent*..."

"A person is either *fat* or *skinny*…"

"Either you *trust* someone or you *don't*."

So a person might look at herself and say, "I am not pretty, so I must be ugly…I am not intelligent, so I must be dumb…I am not skinny, so I must be fat…My boyfriend crossed me one time, so he is completely untrustworthy." Actually, though, there are degrees of attractiveness, intelligence, and size.

```
                    Degrees of Attractiveness

    Totally ---------------------------------------------- Totally
    Ugly                                                   Beautiful

                    Degrees of Intelligence


    Totally ---------------------------------------------- Totally
    Dumb                                                   Intelligent

                            Size


    Totally ---------------------------------------------- Totally
    Skinny                                                 Fat

                    Degrees of Trust


    Totally---------------------------------------------Totally
    Distrust                                            Trust
```

All-or-none thinking often interferes with setting goals and achieving them. People often say, "If I can't earn $100,000 a year, I'm not working at all…" (as if it would not be worth the effort of working to earn $50,000 or $25,000) or "If I can't get an "A" on this test, I'm not going to study…" (as if it would not be worth the effort of studying just to pass, like passing would not be better than failing) or "If I do not find a woman that will treat me exactly the way I want to be treated, I'm not getting married…"(as if having a wife who treats him mostly as he would like to be treated is not beneficial nor better than having no wife at all).

I often hear all-or-none thinking from people trying to lose weight. A very common scenario is something like this:

"I started my diet plan on a Monday. My plan called for me to avoid all sweets, including cookies and candies. I did really well until Thursday. That's when my husband came home with a dozen doughnuts and stuck them on the counter. I looked at those doughnuts and decided that eating one wouldn't hurt me. So I ate one. But then I felt really upset because up to that point I was on my diet, but eating that doughnut meant that I was off the diet. I blew my diet. So I just went ahead and ate the rest of the doughnuts…"

Rather than putting the one doughnut into perspective and realizing that there are degrees to which a person can stray from a diet plan, people often take this type of all-or-none approach.

Perfectionism is an excellent example of all-or-none thinking. "If I can't do it perfectly well, I'm not doing it at all…If every blade of grass in my yard is not the same length, my yard is unacceptable."

Words and expressions that imply all-or-none thinking include:

–"That was a waste of time."
–"It's completely ruined."
–"I blew it."
–"It was destroyed."
–"She is perfect."
–"They completely messed up."

Avoid making the "all-or-none" mistake by considering the possibility of a "middle ground."

(2) <u>Overgeneralization</u>

To overgeneralize is to exaggerate unintentionally. The two words most often used when people overgeneralize are **always** and **never**. These two words are not a problem when they *accurately* describe a situation. For example, if I were to say that as long as my wife and I have been married she has never served me raw fish for dinner, that would be an accurate statement, because she hasn't. However, if she had served it one time in twenty years, the word "never" would not be accurate.

Some people might say, "What's the difference between saying "one time in twenty years" and "never?" You might as well say "never." The difference is that the word "never" can imply inability. For example:

<u>Client</u>: "I never do my job right at work."

<u>Me</u>: "Never?"

<u>Client</u>: "I work on an assembly line, and the other day I put the panel on correctly just once out of 100 times!"

<u>Me</u>: "It sure would have been nice if you had done it correctly more often."

<u>Client</u>: "Yea."

<u>Me</u>: "Well, it sounds like you are exaggerating to yourself, though. You said that you *never* do your job right at work. The fact is you did do it correctly once."

<u>Client</u>: "What's the difference between one time out of 100 and zero times out of 100? I might as well say never!"

<u>Me</u>: "The difference is in what saying "never" implies to you. Your perception that you never do the job properly implies to you that you do not have the potential to do it correctly. If you do not think you have the potential to do well, you will stop trying. However, what does that one time that you got it right prove to you?"

<u>Client</u>: "That I can do it."

<u>Me</u>: "That's right! Now what's important is to see how many more times out of 100 you can do it properly."

Overgeneralization is the *inaccurate* use of the words always and never. An example of the inaccurate use of the word "always" is:

Client: "My boss always yells at me, and I'm darn mad about it…"

Me: "Are you sure he *always* yells at you?"

Client: "Yep. He always yells at me."

Me: "O.K. Well, how often and how long would he yell at you if in fact he *always* yelled at you?"

Client: "Well…I guess he'd yell at me twenty-four hours a day, seven days a week."

Me: "That's right! You and your brain have known since you were very young that always means *constantly, without stopping.* "Always" does *not* mean "sometimes" or "occasionally" or "every now-and-then." Let me ask you. How many days a week does your boss yell at you?"

Client: "Four to five days a week…"

Me: "O.K.. And how many times a day does he yell at you?"

Client: "Usually just once."

Me: "Is this an all-day yelling?"

Client: "No. He yells at me for about two minutes each time. I guess I was exaggerating to myself, huh?"

Me: "Yes. There is a big difference between twenty-four hours a day, seven days a week and two *minutes* a day, five days a week…Is there a difference in how you would feel if you thought, "My boss yells at me much more than I wish he would" and "He always yells at me?"

Therefore, it is very important to make certain that you use the words "always" and "never" accurately. If you do not, you will have an exaggerated response to what is going on.

Another way people overgeneralize is when they take one small sample of something and assume it reflects everything with similar characteristics. Overgeneralization causes prejudice. "All African Americans are bad because *one* beat me up…All Catholics are boozers because *the ones I know* are…All Whites hate anyone that is not like them because *the ones I know* are like that…" These are obvious overgeneralizations that cause us to develop an opinion of someone or something before we have gotten to know them.

Avoid overgeneralizing by taking people and things on a "case-by-case" basis.

(3) Mental Filter

Mental filter is a mental mistake that affects everyone on a daily basis to some degree. Mental filter is the mistake of only seeing or acknowledging information that is consistent or "fits" with what you already think or believe. It is like having blinders on. If information that is contrary to one's belief is seen or acknowledged, it will need to be modified to make it fit. Have you ever wanted to go to Paris in the Spring? I've never been to Paris, but I understand that it is lovely, especially in the Spring. Ah, Paris in the Spring. How wonderful it would be to experience that.

Is that what is written in the above triangle, "Paris in the Spring?" That's what you likely saw if you are familiar with the expression. However, what it actually says is "Paris in the *the* Spring." If you failed to "see" the extra "the," it is because this familiar expression created a mind set that then led you to overlook information that is contrary to it.

If a person had a lifelong tendency of thinking of herself as stupid, she would likely either not be aware of, or forget, evidence that shows that she is intelligent (i.e., she files her own taxes, she graduated from college), or she would modify this information to make it consistent with her belief (i.e., "A moron could do their taxes…" and "My professors were easy on me…I went to an easy school…").

Mental filter plays a role when we fall "in love." When two people meet and fall in love, they develop a mental filter (or blinders) for each other. The female in the heterosexual relationship might think, "He's outstanding, wonderful, and fantastic. There is no one like him. He can do no wrong." So a friend tells her, "Don't date that guy, he is an axe murderer!" She responds by saying, "Oh no, not my Johnnie. There is no way he could be an axe murderer." After being together for a while, they move from a romantic love to a more "mature" love. The partners might love each other even more than they had previously, but the excitement has toned down a little (thankfully, or we would never get anything done!). It is during this time that the partners are likely to say, "You've changed. You are not like how you used to be." While it is true that people do change their behavior over time, what also occurs is that the "blinders" come down, and now they see *all* of each other, not what just fit that very positive notion of each other. By the time they seek marital therapy, she might have another set of blinders that supports the idea, "He can do nothing right!"

Sometimes mental filter is intentional in that a person refuses to acknowledge information contrary to his or her beliefs. Often, though, it is unintentional. Have you ever looked "too hard" for something? You look through a drawer trying to find something, but you do not see it despite the fact that it is right in front of you. That is an example of unintentional mental filter.

The following is a great (but unfortunate) example of unintentional mental filter. It is something that actually happened to me.

When my wife and I lived in a rural area of Southwest Virginia, our best friends were Paul and Linda. They had moved to the area from Florida. Linda was originally from the area. They moved back to Virginia to retire and to build a house on her parents' farm land. They built their house approximately fifty yards from her parents' house.

While living in Virginia, we were blessed with our first child, Aldo, Jr. He was born on a Monday after my wife endured a thirty-six-hour labor. My parents came from the Pittsburgh area to visit their grandchild the following Monday. As we were visiting, my wife decided to take Aldo to the bedroom to nurse him. The phone rang shortly afterwards. It was Paul. He sounded upset. I asked him, "Paul, what is wrong?" Paul said, "Linda's dead." I asked what had happened. He went on to describe that Linda was driving a tractor, and it had tipped over, landed on her, and killed her. I asked Paul if I could do anything to help him. He said he had everything under control, so we ended the conversation.

I had the unfortunate task of telling my wife that her best friend had just died. After I told her, my father suggested that he and I go to Paul's home to see what we could do for him. I agreed. Before we left, I telephoned the church we all had attended to tell the priest that Linda had died.

On our way to Paul's house, my father and I commented on how life stinks. We figured Paul would move back to Florida. When we arrived at his home, we saw him standing on his in-laws' porch waving his arms. So we walked down to meet him, gave him a hug, and he invited us into his in-laws' house.

My father, Paul, and I stood in the kitchen talking when, much to my and my father's surprise, *Linda came walking into the room*! It was like a scene from the Twilight Zone television show. Our mouths literally dropped, and I could not speak. Finally, I said, "Linda, I thought you died!" She said, "I didn't die, my *dad* died." What Paul had said on the telephone was "**Linda's *dad***," but I thought that he had said, "**Linda's *dead*!**" So although Paul was telling me how Linda's father was on the tractor and how he was killed, I placed her on the tractor, and that is all I heard.

While we certainly were sad for Linda that her father had died, we were happy that she was still with us.

So I then *quite hesitantly* called my wife to tell her that her best friend had not died. She was ready to kill me! As we were talking on the phone, I looked out the window, and, much to my dismay, I saw a bus load of people from the church coming up the driveway all thinking Linda had died! They continue to tease me to this day about the day Linda died!

I wish that I had I asked one very simple question, "Paul, what was Linda doing on a tractor?" I could have avoided making this mistake had I done so, as I had never known her to ride a tractor.

What can you do about mental filter?

Sometimes people will tell me, "There is nothing good in my life…My life totally stinks!" This belief is usually the result of having a very narrow view of their life experience. When we ask them to look at all aspects of their life intentionally, they often come up with the following:

My Life

Bad	Good
Job Stinks, Wife Nags	Good Health, Enjoy the Children, Close Friends,
Leaky Roof, Bills,	Wife is Very Attractive, Eat Well, Sleep Well,
Boss Yelling at Me,	Fishing Every Saturday, Have A Nice House,
I'm Short & Fat,	Live in a Nice Neighborhood, Have a Good
I'm Going Bald…	Education, Can Feed Myself, Have No Difficulty
	Breathing, Walk Well, Have All the Strength
	I Need, My Children Love Me, Nice Car,
	Have the Potential to Do A Lot of Things,
	Enjoy Going to Church……….

Naturally, if *all* a person looks at is the bad, he will not see the good. This is not to suggest that it does not make sense to acknowledge the "bad" to see what can be done to change it. It is best to look at all aspects of a situation when assessing it.

Part of the problem with the mental mistake of mental filter is that we naturally pay attention to information that supports the way we think and discard information that does not. When is the last time you woke up in the morning saying to yourself, "I think that I'll try to prove myself wrong today?" If you are like most people, you probably have never said that to yourself!

Amateur Attorney Technique

A key to overcoming mental filter is to intentionally, forcefully looking for evidence that supports a different way of thinking.

What I call the Amateur Attorney Technique is a simple way to look for new evidence. First, develop a new belief, one that you do not necessarily completely believe yet, but that does pass the Rational Questions. Then pretend that you are an attorney and have to defend this belief in court. It is your job to convince the jury that this new belief is accurate. You have one week to prepare your case. For the next week, write down everything that you can think of that will support your case. You need not believe that the information actually does support the new idea (attorneys sometimes say things they do not believe in defense of their clients). However, refuse to fabricate or "make up" evidence. Provide actual examples.

For example, if I'm working with a client who thinks of herself as "dumb" (she actually uses the word), but I have reason to believe that she is at least of average intelligence, I would ask her to consider adopting the new belief, "I am at least of average intelligence." I then would ask the client to pretend that she is an attorney and that she has been hired to defend this belief in court. It is her job to convince the jury that she is at least of average intelligence. She has until the next session to prepare her case. For the next week, she is to write down everything that she can think of that will support her case.

I *can be incorrect* in my thinking!

Adopting this attitude also is very helpful in overcoming mental filter. Not only *can* I be wrong in my thinking, sometimes I *hope* I'm wrong! What thoughts do you think about yourself, others, and the world around you that you hope are incorrect? Hoping that you might be incorrect, and realizing it is possible, will help you to be motivated to look for evidence that you just might be mistaken!

(4) Discounting the Positive

The mental mistake of "discounting the positive" works hand-in-hand with mental filter. People discount the positive to support their negative belief. (Note, however, that people also often discount negative information to support positive beliefs.)

For example, as a person depresses himself, he tends to discount the positive in his life. If this continues, he might get to the point where he believes that *nothing* in life is good. Another example is a person believing that receiving an "A" on a test means that the teacher felt sorry for him, that the test was easy, or that anyone could have obtained a similar result. This assumption helps him continue to believe that he is stupid ("stupid people do not make 'A's' on tests").

Rational thinking is based on fact. Sometimes facts are personally positive, sometimes they are personally negative. Acknowledging *all* of the facts is important, not just those that support our beliefs.

(5) Jumping to Conclusions

Jumping to conclusions is developing an opinion about something very quickly without gathering facts. The fact that we tend to do this very quickly is the reason we call it *jumping* to conclusions. Sometimes people jump to conclusions because it is easier than gathering facts. That is why one of my favorite comedians, Stephen Wright, says, "A conclusion is what you come to when you get tired of thinking about something." There is a lot of truth in that statement! We are working at developing endurance for thinking—a willingness to gather facts.

The two most common ways people jump to conclusions are **mind reading** and **fortune telling**.

Mind Reading

Mind reading is just what the name implies—acting as if we can read other peoples' minds. However, mind reading is *not*, "He *might* be thinking this…" or "She *might* be thinking that…" Mind reading is "I *know* he is thinking…" and then *acting* on that so-called knowledge.

The **first problem** with mind reading is that we cannot read peoples' minds! While there are machines that show us that a person *is* thinking (an electroencephalogram), no instrument can tell us *what* a person is thinking (although one probably will be invented some day). Not even the psychics can tell us what a person is thinking. Frankly, I say, "Thank God!" Could you imagine the trouble we would have if we could read minds? We would have far more trouble than we already do!

Some people justify mind reading by stating, "When you know someone as long as I have, you know how they think." However, no matter how well you know someone, you cannot know what they think. The more familiar we are with a person the better we are at predicting how they will act, react, and the statements they are likely to make in a given situation. However, familiarity does not, in any way, give us the ability to see inside the person's brain to read his or her mind.

Acting on information "gathered" by mind reading can lead to trouble. For example, imagine that Bill comes home two hours late from work. As he enters his home, he notices that his wife, Sue, has a certain look on her face. He says to himself, "She looks like she is mad, and I just know she's mad at me because I'm late. I hate it when she's mad at me for being late, because she knows it's the nature of my job. Because she's mad at me, I'll be mad right back!" So Bill proceeds to yell at her. After he is finished yelling, Sue says, "Bill, I wasn't mad at you before you began yelling at me, but now I am! What you saw on my face was pain because my back has been hurting all day." As a result, Bill's mind-reading error would have led to a completely avoidable argument. How could he have avoided this argument? Bill could have seen his wife's facial expression and said to himself, "Sue looks like she's mad, but I don't know for sure, so I'll ask her." This approach would have given Sue an opportunity to explain her facial expression and, therefore, to avoid an argument.

We certainly do observe others from time to time and make certain assumptions of what they are thinking based on how they are acting. It is important, though, to view these assumptions as *guesses* as opposed to thoughts that necessary are based on fact.

For those that are particularly hardheaded about mind reading, believing that they have the ability, I pose the following supposition. Suppose that I asked you to give me $100. I tell you that if you can guess which number I am thinking of that is between one and four, I'll give you $200. If you do not correctly guess which number, I can keep your $100. Without me writing the number down, or telling someone else, would you take the chance that:

(1) you could correctly guess which number I selected, and

(2) that I would be honest enough to tell you if in fact you had guessed it correctly?

If I told you that your guess was incorrect, there would be no way that you could prove that you actually were correct or that I am lying. Would you be willing to take this chance of losing $100? I'll bet not!

The **second problem** with attempting to read minds is that it is pointless. What other people *think* is irrelevant. It simply does not affect us one way or another. What does matter to us is how they *act, how they treat us*. A person could think as much as he wanted that he wants to shoot me. As long as he does not act on that thought, I have no problem. If he were to act on that thought, that probably would ruin my day! Conversely, a person could think that she would love to give me a part of her financial fortune, but if she does not act on that thought, I will not benefit from it.

If you are being treated in a way that is unpleasant to you, rather than trying to figure out what someone must be thinking, discuss the matter with them and see if they are willing to treat you differently.

Fortune Telling

Fortune telling is jumping to conclusions by predicting the future. As with mind reading, fortune telling is *not* thinking, "This *might* happen…" Fortune telling is, "I *know* it is going to happen," then acting on that so-called knowledge.

Examples of fortune telling include: "I just know I'm going to flunk the test, so I'm not going to study…If I ask my boss for a raise, he will tell me no…My parents are really going to be upset over this one…"

Granted, the more familiar we are with a situation or person, the better we will tend to be at *predicting* future events. However, no future event is certain to occur (except death). There is nothing irrational about making educated predictions for personal guidance. For example, a person might extensively research market demand and determine that marketing a product would very likely produce a large profit. A rational decision to invest money into the project would take into account the significance of his research findings.

People often shape the future based on their *predictions* of it. The belief, "I just know I'm going to flunk the test, so I'm not going to study," could lead to a **self-fulfilling prophecy**. A self-fulfilling prophecy is the result of people unintentionally creating the predicted outcome because they predicted it. Believing that he knows that he will flunk a test would lead a person not to study for it. After taking the test and flunking it, he likely would say, "You see, I *told* you I wouldn't pass the test!" It is clear to see, however, that his not studying *might have been what led to his flunking the test!* Had he made a guess that he would not pass, but decided to study nevertheless, the outcome *might* have been different.

Here is an example of a very common scenario involving fortune telling.

Client: "I got a low grade on my math test the other day. I sure wish I could bring up my grade."

Me: "How about asking your teacher if you could do some extra credit?"

Client: "There is no point in asking her."

Me: "Why not?"

Client: "Because I know that she will tell me no."

Me: "How do you know that?"

Client: "I just know it."

Me: (Getting out a piece of paper and marker, I draw a crystal ball with the word "no" in it.) "You see, what you are telling me is that you have a crystal ball that can tell you exactly what will happen in the future. Now I'm sure that you'll agree that you do not have a crystal ball showing us that she will say no, and I do not have a crystal ball showing us that she will say yes. Would you agree with that?"

Client: "Yes."

Me: "Okay. Now, what makes it seem to you that she is likely to say no."

Client: "Because she has said no to everyone that I know has asked her, and that's about everyone in the class."

Me: "Okay, so if we had to bet a lot of money whether or not she will tell you no when you ask her, given what you have told me, we probably would bet that she would tell you no, right?"

Client: "Yea."

<u>Me</u>: "However, since we do not have a crystal ball to tell us for certain that she will say no, no matter how many times she has denied other students in the past, let me ask you. What do you have to lose by asking her, anyway?"

<u>Client</u>: "She might yell at me."

<u>Me</u>: "Okay. Well, I do not know of anyone that enjoys being yelled at. How important is it to you that you bring your grade up?"

<u>Client</u>: "Very important."

<u>Me</u>: "O.k. Then let me ask you this. Have you ever been yelled at before?"

<u>Client</u>: "Sure."

<u>Me</u>: "Did you survive it?"

<u>Client</u>: "I didn't like it!"

<u>Me</u>: "I'm sure, but did you survive it?"

<u>Client</u>: "I guess so. I'm still alive."

<u>Me</u>: "That's right. Now might it be worth taking the chance that you might get yelled at to see if your teacher would be willing to give you an extra credit assignment?"

<u>Client</u>: "I guess so, yea."

To avoid jumping to conclusions, take your time to formulate your opinions and consider all the facts.

(6) <u>Magnification</u>

Magnification is the mental mistake of exaggerating the importance of a shortcoming or minimizing the importance of a good quality. For example, teenagers often take this approach when it comes to acne! "This is a *world-record-sized* pimple…everyone at the party will look at it, so I'm not going to go…" is the approach some take to their acne problem. Or a law student might minimize the importance of her intelligence and knowledge and insist that she will not be an effective attorney because she lisps. Although her law professors tell her that she has a great deal of potential, she believes that her potential "doesn't count" and, instead, focuses on the lisping.

To avoid magnifying, ask yourself:

(1) Is this shortcoming really likely to interfere with achieving my goals?

(2) Does my shortcoming really affect my life the way I think it does?

(3) Might my strengths affect my situation more than my shortcomings?

Magnification is sometimes related to the "too much/too little" problem that we'll discuss later in this chapter.

(7) <u>Emotional Reasoning</u>

Emotional reasoning is thinking that is affected by emotions—how you are feeling at the time. For example, when a person is depressed about one thing, he or she is likely to think depressing thoughts about other things as well—things about which he or she ordinarily would not think pessimistically. This mind-set can become quite pessimistic, and the more pessimistic it becomes, the more depressed the person becomes (a vicious circle).

Sometimes our physical feelings influence our reasoning as well. We certainly know how fatigue can lead us to be less tolerant of situations. We often do not deal as well with problems when we are ill, sometimes viewing them as more significant or difficult than they actually are.

To avoid emotional reasoning, first identify it as such. Because you have been paying attention to your thinking, you are becoming increasingly aware of your typical ways of thinking when you are calm (which is usually more representative of how you actually think). When your thoughts are contrary to your typical ways of thinking, determine your **mood** and ask yourself if your thinking is how you really think, or if it is a reflection of the mood you are in. Ask yourself:

Do I think this way about (current situation) when I'm not already upset about something else?

If not, refuse to take seriously the thought produced through emotional reasoning.

(8) <u>Irrational Labeling</u>

Labeling is assigning a name to something. Labeling is necessary for communication—we could not communicate without it. For the request, "Please get me a glass of water" to be responded to properly, one must understand what a "glass" is and what "water" is.

However, labeling can be a problem when a label is inaccurate and/or when it limits our view of ourselves or others. Labels can encourage the creation of a self-fulfilling prophecy. People can unintentionally create the very condition or situation they predict because of how they label themselves or others. If a person labels himself (or accepts the label from others) "delinquent," he is likely to act out the part. What else would a person expect from a "delinquent" but delinquent behavior?

Inaccurate Labels

Inaccurate labeling is assigning a word or phrase to something that does not accurately describe it. Inaccurate labels take many forms, as the following example demonstrates:

<u>Client</u>: "I am just a stupid idiot."

<u>Me</u>: "Why do you say that?"

<u>Client</u>: "Because I make a lot of mistakes."

<u>Me</u>: "Well, the first problem is that you are labeling yourself a stupid idiot. Now, if I were to take a picture of you and take it home to my wife, she would not say, "What a nice picture of a stupid idiot!"

<u>Client</u>: (Laughing) "No, I guess not."

<u>Me</u>: "That's right. She would see a person in the picture and maybe wonder who it is. Now I'm sure that you are aware that some dictionaries have pictures next to some words to illustrate the meaning of the word, right?"

<u>Client</u>: "Yea."

<u>Me</u>: "If we were to look up the word 'idiot' in the dictionary, would there be a picture next to the word?"

<u>Client</u>: "No, I don't think there would be."

<u>Me</u>: "That's right, and the reason is that there is no objectively identifiable thing as an idiot! There are *people* that might *act in an idiotic way*, but that describes just about everyone from time to time, doesn't it?"

<u>Client</u>: "It sure does! But I act idiotically more often than others."

<u>Me</u>: "Well, we'll need to take a look at that to see if that's the case. Even if you do act idiotically more often than others, that still only makes you a *person* who has acted idiotically more often than others, not an "idiot." Plus, if there were such a creature as a stupid idiot, what would that creature only be capable of?"

<u>Client</u>: "I guess acting idiotically and that's it."

<u>Me</u>: "Now, do you know anyone that is actually like that?"

<u>Client</u>: "No, I sure don't."

<u>Me</u>: "Now there are people who have very low intellectual levels. But they are *people* with low intelligence, *not idiots or retards!* So I encourage you to refrain from labeling yourself anything but an FHB. Have I described what an FHB is to you yet?"

<u>Client</u>: "No, I don't believe you have."

<u>Me</u>: "FHB stands for Fallible Human Being, meaning that you are a human being and you make mistakes, just like everyone else. Therefore, any word or phrase that follows the words "I'm a _____" that isn't 'Fallible Human Being' just is not accurate."

People in our society tend to use many labels that do not accurately describe themselves and others. The consequences of the use of inaccurate labels include unwanted emotional upset and a limited view of ourselves and others.

A limited view of oneself and others can have a serious impact on how we treat ourselves and others. Vice President Dan Quayle was an unfortunate recipient of negative labeling. Quayle was, in effect, labeled an "idiot" by many people in our society, and the media seemed to treat him as such. Their "idiot" label so limited peoples' view of him that Quayle could have had the answer to all of the nation's problems, but no one would have seen it as such, because "idiots do not say intelligent things."

Narrowing Our View of Ourselves and Others

Common Labels include depressed person, lucky person, fat person, angry person, alcoholic, criminal, murderer, accountant, lawyer, doctor, electrician, father, mother, and molester. Remember, though, that there is no such thing as a "depressed person," but rather a *person* who has made himself depressed. There is no such thing as a doctor, but rather a *person* who practices medicine for a living.

The following example demonstrates the importance of making such a distinction.

<u>Client</u>: "My husband couldn't do the wiring for the house because he's an accountant."

<u>Me</u>: "Why would his being an accountant keep him from doing the house wiring?"

Client: "Because he's an accountant…What would he know about wiring?"

Me: "Well, first of all, he is not an accountant…He is a person who does accounting for a living…Therefore, since he is a person, there is the possibility that he might know wiring in addition to accounting. If there were such a thing as an accountant, all this thing would know is accounting. But I imagine he knows other things besides accounting, doesn't he?"

Client: "Sure…I see what you mean…I guess I had him kind of typecasted, didn't I?"

Me: "That's right, and this typecasting is called labeling."

Remember, if the sentence, "I am a _____," or "He/she is a _____," does not end with "human being" or "fallible human being," the sentence does not accurately describe you or others.

(9) Personalization & Blame

The mental mistake of personalization and blame occurs when a person inaccurately assumes the cause of something. Sometimes it is blaming someone or something for a situation when in fact they in no way caused it. Other times it is blaming someone or something *too* much when in fact other factors were responsible as well. Problems associated with making this mental mistake include:

a) **Guilt**, because you think that what went wrong was all your fault, and you "shouldn't" have done what you did to cause it;

b) **Resentment**, because you think that what went wrong was all someone else's fault, and they shouldn't have done what they did to cause it; and

c) **Trying to change the wrong thing**. It is like thinking that the reason your car is stalling is because you have a bad fuel pump when in fact your camshaft is bad. Rather than changing the camshaft, you will naturally change the fuel pump, only to find that the car continues to stall.

It is important for us to accurately assess the cause of a problem to correct it. We cause our own upset and behaviors through *our own thinking*. Other people's behaviors are caused by *their thoughts*, not by us, although we might encourage them to think or act a certain way. When it comes to interpersonal relationships, rarely is conflict the fault of a single person.

Sometimes misinformation or a lack of information leads to personalization and blame. This misinformation encourages a person to jump to conclusions about what the cause of an undesirable situation *must* have been.

For example, parents tend to blame themselves for their children's problematic behavior. If a twenty-five-year-old son has been arrested for drug possession, his parents might jump to the conclusion that they must have done something wrong in raising him. While they might have done things to encourage their son to commit criminal acts, he would have had to *decide to act* on those suggestions or teachings to commit such acts. Additionally, many different sources influence children growing up, including parents, siblings, teachers, friends, songs, television, and printed material. Therefore, it is quite unrealistic for parents to believe that they were, or should have been, the only influence in the child's life.

Do your best to assess the cause(s) of problematic situations accurately. You can attribute the cause of an event to someone or something *without angrily blaming them*. Usually you are more likely to receive their cooperation when you calmly express your concerns.

(10) <u>Irrational Should Statements</u>

Irrational should statements cause anger and guilt. When we are angry with someone, we are pointing a "should" in their direction ("You should not treat me that way."). When we feel guilty, we are pointing the "should" inward, as guilt is anger turned inward.

Should statements are irrational when they are in the form of moralistic demands, commands, and rules, and when they imply a belief in magic.

Moralistic Use of Should

Most people use the word "should" to express a rule, demand, or command. "A husband should take out the garbage…A wife should do the laundry…A child should respect his or her parents…You should not steal…" These should statements are also expressed as *musts*, *have-to's*, and *ought-to's*. They are usually absolute rules, and violating them supposedly produces dire consequences.

Many "shoulds" are societal rules. Having rules is important for a society, otherwise there would be chaos. However, many societal rules are not based on fact, but are simply made up and then followed blindly. Nevertheless, we believe them because we do not know *not* to, as the following example demonstrates:

<u>Client</u>: "I felt so lazy and thought of myself as good-for-nothing the other day…"

<u>Me</u>: "Why?"

<u>Client</u>: "Because I didn't do the dishes immediately after I ate."

<u>Me</u>: "Why would you think of yourself as lazy and good-for-nothing when you don't do the dishes immediately after eating?"

<u>Client</u>: "Because a person *should* do the dishes after they eat."

<u>Me</u>: "Who told you that?"

<u>Client</u>: "My mother preached that to me…"

<u>Me</u>: "O.K. Who do you think taught your mother that rule?"

<u>Client</u>: "I guess her mother did…"

<u>Me</u>: "Yea, probably so…So if we kept searching for the originator of that rule, we might find a group of people that deemed themselves experts on laziness that agreed that if one does not wash the dishes after they eat, he or she is lazy. So now you, and many other people as well, blindly follow this belief as if it were based on fact."

<u>Client</u>: "I see what you mean…"

<u>Me</u>: "Good. Now. Where is the evidence that a person is lazy and good-for-nothing if he or she doesn't do the dishes immediately after eating?"

<u>Client</u>: "I guess there is none, really…"

Me: "Well, when does a person have to do the dishes? When there are no other clean dishes in the house, he or she refuses or is unable to buy more clean dishes, and he or she wants to eat on a clean plate. Now, there usually are advantages to washing the dishes immediately after eating, such as the chore is completed and you can focus on other, more pleasurable things. But would you say that you are good-for-nothing, that you serve no purpose on this Earth?"

Client: (Laughing) "No, I am important to my family and friends."

Me: "That's right. So it is important to refuse to blindly accept societal rules and to sometimes challenge them by looking for the evidence."

Believe it or not, there is a society that to this day believes that a husband should never eat with his wife's side of the family. The belief is that the wife's side of the family is possessed by the devil, and the act of eating makes a person more susceptible to being possessed. Therefore, a man has a much greater chance of being possessed if he eats with his in-laws. While many men throughout the world might agree with this tribe's beliefs, obviously there are no facts to support them! However, if a man in the tribe were to eat with his in-laws, he would be viewed as seriously mentally ill.

We are taught that many things are requirements when in fact they are only preferences. You will learn more about this fact later in my description of "need vs. want." While a person has a right to his or her morals, values, and preferences, the rigid musts, shoulds, and have-to's cause problems. These rigid rules make it difficult to adapt to circumstances that do not adhere to them. Many of these rules are actually good, *recommended practices*. It is recommended that one wash the dishes after one eats as he or she can then focus on other, more pleasurable activities. For the most part, though, the world would not cease to exist if we were not to follow these recommended practices, although it *seems* as though it would when we state them as shoulds, musts, and have-to's.

I encourage you to challenge "should," "musts," and "have-to's" by asking, "*Must* it be this way? How did I come to believe that it must be this way to begin with?"

Magical Aspect of "Should"

Irrational should statements sometimes make it seem as though we believe in magic. If I were to place ingredients together to make a chocolate cake, put it in the oven to let it bake, then take it out of the oven only to discover that I forgot to include the chocolate, *should* the result be a chocolate cake or something other than a chocolate cake? If I were to say that it *should* be a chocolate cake regardless, I would be insisting that the cake be a chocolate cake despite the fact that I didn't include the chocolate. If I forgot to place the chocolate in the mixture, but pulled a chocolate cake out of the oven nevertheless, that would be magic!

Everything is as it should be at any given moment, although it might not be the way we want it to be. For a situation to occur, everything that is necessary for it to occur must be present, or it will not happen. Irrational should statements do not consider reality. Irrational should statements insist that reality conform to one's desires or demands, rather than our desires conforming to reality.

Imagine the following scenario. The NFL Super Bowl has just concluded, and the final score is:

Team A: 37 Points   Team B: 36 Points.

Reporters then interview both head coaches. Team A's coach says, "I am so proud of my boys…They played a terrific game…" Team B's coach says, "We should have won that game." In fact, though, Team B *should have lost* the game.

Obviously, what was necessary for Team B to win wasn't done, or they would have won! Unless the rules of football have changed, the team with the most points at the end of the game wins! If Team B's coach thinks that they *should* have won when what was necessary for them to win *was not done*, his belief would imply a belief in magic. His "should" would imply, "We did everything necessary to win, but somehow magically lost…It was just a fluke that we lost…" By thinking this way, would you expect the coach to make any changes in his game plan for the next time they play each other? I would not! Instead, if he says to himself, "As much as I wish we *would* have won, and although we had the *potential* to win, we *should* have lost because something went wrong for us to end the game with fewer points than our opponent," he would be in a much better position to calmly accept that fact, to determine what actually went wrong, and to correct it.

Accepting your current reality is difficult if you do not acknowledge what that reality is. A benefit of accepting your current reality is that doing so places you in a better position to do something about it. The irrational use of the word "should" causes us to ignore the fact that all the necessary ingredients to create our undesirable situation are all present. Ignoring that fact makes it difficult to change the situation by removing those necessary ingredients.

In other words, if I say, "My boss shouldn't yell at me," I am ignoring the fact that (1) my boss has it in his head to yell at me, and (2) I am there to take it. As long as those two facts are reality, it would be magic for me *not* to get yelled at. For me to stop getting yelled at, either (1) my boss has to change the way he thinks, or (2) I need to remove myself from the situation so that I am not around him to take it.

So everything is as it should be at any given moment because all of the necessary ingredients are there to make it that way. This statement does *not* imply that it is morally right or advantageous that the situation is as it is. The statement simply acknowledges the reality of the situation. Our mere desire for a situation to be a certain way will not make it that way. However, it *should* only be the way we want it to be if all the necessary ingredients are present, *regardless* of whether we whine, cry, hold our breath, or stomp our feet.

When it comes to angering ourselves with irrational should statements, if the anger we feel serves no useful purpose, and we know that the situation will remain the same despite our anger, we might as well calmly accept it. Our calm acceptance of a situation does not mean that we like it or have no desire to change it. Calm acceptance means that you acknowledge the reality of the situation, and, by doing so, are in a much better position to do what is possible to change it.

The Serenity Prayer is based on the principle of calm acceptance:

> *God Grant me The Serenity*
> *to accept things I cannot change,*
> *The Courage to change the things I can, and*
> *The Wisdom to know the difference.*

Work at changing irrational "should" statements to "wish" statements.

Change Irrational "Should" Statements to "Wish" Statements

Irrational "Should"	Rational "Wish"
1. He should have more respect for me.	1. I wish he would have more respect for me, but he doesn't. Let me see what I can do to encourage him to develop more respect for me.
2. She shouldn't treat me like a baby.	2. I wish she wouldn't treat me like a baby, but she does. Let me see what I can do to encourage her to treat me like an adult.
3. I should have known that he would not like it.	3. I wish I would have known that he would not like it, but obviously I didn't. I'll see why I didn't know that and work at doing better next time.
4. I shouldn't have yelled at her.	4. I wish I would not have yelled at her. Obviously, though, I did everything necessary to yell at her, or I would not have. I'll work at removing those necessary ingredients.

Remember…Anger is like urinating in your pants…

Everyone can see it, but you are the only one that can feel it.

So Refuse to "Should All Over Yourself!"

(11) Confusing Needs with Wants

If I were limited to being able to write about only one mental mistake in this chapter, the confusion of needs and wants would be the mistake that I would select. It is by far the most important mental mistake of all described in this chapter.

In Rational Living Therapy, we differentiate between **"absolute needs"** and **wants**. Our **absolute needs** are those things we need to remain alive:

Our Absolute Needs

Those things that are
necessary to remain alive:

Air	Sufficient Warmth
Food	
	Sometimes a
Water	Certain Medication

Everything else on this Earth is a want! However, when we mislabel a "want" as being a "need," we feel just as bad as if we were going without air or food. A very small sample of "wants" that people tend to mislabel as being "needs" includes:

Some of the things we are taught we "need" but actually only "want"

(1) Love from others	(9) To have things go our way
(2) Respect	(10) That new car
(3) Attention	(11) To be treated "well" by others
(4) Confidence	(12) Peace of mind
(5) To have a certain appearance	(13) Perfect health
(6) To have an outstanding job	(14) Outstanding Accomplishments
(7) To have an outstanding education	(15) Perfection
(8) To be liked by everybody	(16) A specific person or group of people

"Need" Statements Cause Anxiety and Anger

Sometimes "need" statements cause anxiety and panic. Imagine how you would feel if you were trapped in a room and you knew that in the next five minutes all of the air in the room would be removed through a vent. You most likely would begin to panic, and the closer it got to the end of the five-minute period, the more anxious you would be. Why? **Because you know that you *need* air to live.** Contrast that example with a situation where you discover that your local grocery store stopped offering your favorite breakfast cereal. You might feel disappointed, but you would not panic like in the first example, **because you know that you only *want* your favorite breakfast cereal,** you do not need it (although you do need food), and that is the difference between needing and wanting.

Sometimes "need" statements cause intense anger. Now imagine how you would feel if you were in a room and you knew that in the next five minutes all of the air in the room would be removed through a vent. However, this time, leaving the room is easy, but I am going to do my best to keep you from getting out. No matter how well you liked me previously, you would make yourself pretty angry at me. Why? **Because I would be keeping you from something that you need—air!**

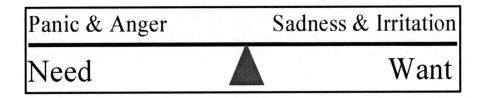

A technique to determine whether something is a need is to ask yourself:

How long can I go without this before I die?

In other words, how long can you go without out it before doing so would kill you? We know approximately how long we could survive without food, air, and water. How long could we *survive* without that new stereo, that boyfriend or girlfriend, or the respect of others? Notice that this is different that killing oneself. When a person commits suicide, *something* does not kill the person—*the person* kills himself or herself.

Conditional Need Statements

"Conditional need statements" are based on an assumption that for Event A to occur, Conditions 1, 2, and 3 must exist. Conditional need statements can be accurate or inaccurate. For example, an *accurate* conditional need would be:

"For me to be physically present at the grocery store, I need to travel to it."

It is impossible for a person to be somewhere without traveling to the destination. An *inaccurate* conditional need would be:

"For me to be happy, I need to have $1,000,000."

If a person believes that there is no other possible way to be happy other than to have one million dollars, he or she will act as if that were the case. Obviously, there are other ways to make oneself happy.

Sometimes "absolute need" statements are hidden within "conditional need" statements. For example, an accurate "conditional need" statement is, "For Joe to obtain a legitimate college degree, he needs to complete a college program." However, if he does not get accepted into a college program and panics in response, he would be equating his failing to obtain a college degree with a life-or-death situation (absolute need).

But don't we need someone to love us?

I am asked this question routinely, especially by therapists who attend my seminars. It is a difficult question to answer, because we must first *define* love to be able to decide whether we need it. If I were to ask each reader to send to me their definition of food, water, and air, I would receive pretty consistent definitions. They would all be about the same. However, if I were to ask for definitions of love, I would receive many different definitions.

I cannot think of anything that would be included in a definition of love that is something that we need, but I can think of many things that we might want. For example, a common definition of love includes conditions, such as, "when people love you, they hug you, kiss you, tell you that they love you, they take care of you when you are not feeling well, etc.... " These conditions or elements of the definition are wants or desires, not needs. People do not die from a lack of hugs, kisses, or verbal affection. Most (not all) people want those things, but they are not needs. Actually, that fact alone proves they are not needs. Everyone needs to have air, food, and water, but not everyone wants love, affection, and attention.

Sometimes therapists use as proof that we need love the fact that years ago babies died in orphanages, and their deaths were attributed to a "lack of love." It turns out, though, that what they likely died from was a lack of tactile stimulation—caretakers did not touch them enough. It might be that infants need tactile stimulation, but adults do not appear to have such a need. Nevertheless, a person does not need to love someone to provide tactile stimulation.

(12) Confusing Choosing to (Choice) with Having To (Force)

Anytime people have the sincere impression that they are forced to do something they do not want to do, they resent it. The more that they dislike it, and the greater the perception of being forced, the greater the resentment.

The only time we are ever *forced* to do something is when we are physically overpowered and made to do against our will. Otherwise, when we do something, no matter how much we dislike doing it, we are *choosing* or *deciding* to do it.

Sometimes when we decide to do something, it is because it is the lesser of two evils. For example, every time we file and pay our income taxes, we choose or decide to do so. Why? Because choosing *not* to pay them leads to a consequence that is unacceptable to us. Could we tell the Internal Revenue Service what to do with their 1040 form? Sure we could! Some people do! However, paying our taxes, as unpleasant as most of us view it, is not as unpleasant as are the consequences of not paying them!

Realizing that we are deciding to do something rather than being forced to significantly reduces our resentment. It does not make the event or duty more appealing. It does make our experience with it more pleasant, though.

Also, realizing that we are deciding to do something rather than being forced to places us in a position to take credit for having made a wise decision.

For example, many people resent the process of dieting because they view themselves as "having to" diet and "having to" lose weight. Perhaps they *need* to lose weight to fit into a particular bathing suit or to lessen their risk of heart disease, but *they do not have to* fit in the bathing suit or lessen their risk of heart disease. Those are optional things to do. Actually, people choose to diet for many different reasons. When people realize that it is their *choice* that leads them to diet, and they also realize that at any time they can *choose* to return to previous eating habits, they feel much better about their dieting and are usually much more willing to do so.

A basic fact of life is that the *only* thing we *have to do* is die. Ultimately, dying is absolutely *un*avoidable. Everything else is optional.

Keep yourself mindful of the difference between "choosing to" and "having to," and you will lessen your frustration and resentment level considerably.

(13) Can't Stand-itis

Can't Stand-itis is an extension of the confusion of needing and wanting.

Can't Stand-itis is another form of underestimating one's ability to tolerate a situation. Severe can't stand-itis implies a belief that one *needs* a situation to be different than it is. When we view a situation or condition as something we cannot stand, we tend to avoid it as if *not* doing so would kill us. Conversely, when we believe that we have the ability to deal with or to tolerate a situation effectively, we tend to be unafraid to approach it.

The following is a typical example of "can't stand-itis" in action and how to dispute it.

Client: "My daughter has been hanging around the wrong crowd and getting into trouble with drugs. I want her to stop, so when she disobeys me about it I make her to stay at home, usually for one week. But every time I ground her, I end up letting her go back out after one hour."

Me: "Why do you do that?"

Client: "Because she starts yelling at me and calling me all sorts of names."

<u>Me</u>: "Okay, but why would you let her outside when you are trying to correct her behavior?"

<u>Client</u>: "Because *I can't stand it* when she yells at me and calls me names."

<u>Me</u>: "Well, I do not know anyone that enjoys being yelled at. With that said, I'll bet you that you can stand it. I'll bet you my house, my practice, and what little saving I have because of my house and practice…I'll even throw in my children and bet you that you can stand it when your daughter yells at you."

<u>Client</u>: "How can you say that?"

<u>Me</u>: "Because you are sitting here telling me about it. If you couldn't stand your daughter yelling at you, you would have died. Now if you were to tell me that you couldn't stand a piano falling on your head, I'd say you probably would be right. But when you tell your brain that you cannot stand your daughter yelling at you, how do you act?"

<u>Client</u>: "Like her yelling at me is going to kill me!"

<u>Me</u>: "Exactly! Beautiful! Granted, I'm sure that you do not like being yelled at. Most of us don't. But if you view your daughter's yelling at you as being what it actually is—an inconvenience, you will simply make yourself irritated and annoyed, rather than very anxious and angry. Now, if you were to be simply irritated and annoyed, what do you think you would do when she yells at you?"

<u>Client</u>: "Stick to my guns and keep her in the house."

<u>Me</u>: "That's right."

Unless it is something that can kill you, replace the statement, "I can't stand it" with "I don't like it, and because I don't like it, I'm going to do something about it."

A Special Note: What about the quality of life?

Occasionally, I am asked about the importance of the quality of life. A client might ask, "Yea I know what's going on won't kill me, but what about being happy?" To understand the answer to this question, allow me first to explain what is known as "Maslow's Hierarchy of Needs."

Abraham Maslow (1954) identified what he described as "innate needs" as "needs" that when fulfilled provide satisfaction and meaning to a person's life. These "needs" make the person experience a constant "deficit state." Just as one need is satisfied, another need "kicks in" placing the person in a position of always striving for something. Maslow demonstrated how these "needs" are prioritized into a hierarchy as follows:

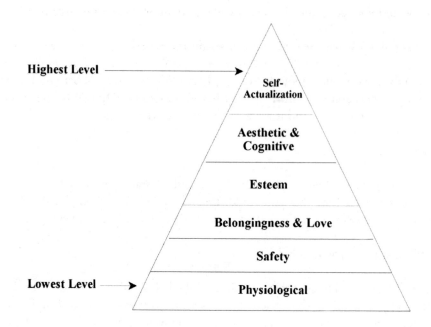

Abraham Maslow's (1954) Hierarchy of "Needs"

For a person to be concerned with a higher-level need, he or she must first have the lower-level needs generally satisfied. For example, if a person is starving (a physiological need to eat), she is not going to be very concerned about her self-esteem at that moment. If a person is in a war zone with bombs exploding around him (safety needs), he is not going to be concerned about his awareness of knowledge or about writing poetry (aesthetic & cognitive needs).

From a Rational Living Therapy perspective, though, the only true "needs" among those listed in Maslow's hierarchy are the physiological. To live, we need to have our physical needs met. The remainder of what Maslow describes as needs are actually wants—things we sometimes desire to make life better or to add quality to our lives.

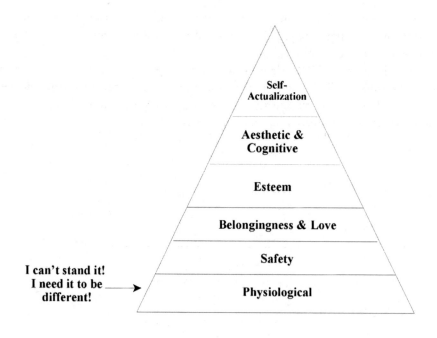

By the way, the "Safety" needs are a *sense* of safety. People do not need to have a sense of safety, but we need to be safe to remain alive (physiological need).

When we mistakenly believe that we cannot stand something, we subsequently act as though we are going to die, as if a physiological need is not being met. So thinking or acting as though we can't stand something or that we need a situation to be different than it is puts us on the physiological level of the hierarchy. As long as that perception exists, we are not going to care about those things that bring quality to our lives, like being loved, belonging to a group, esteeming ourselves, etc.…

(14) <u>Catastrophizing</u>

Catastrophizing is another form of underestimating one's potential to deal with a situation effectively. This underestimation often leads us to viewing the situation as worse than it actually is for us.

Words and expressions often used when catastrophizing are: awful, terrible, horrible, catastrophic, and end-of-the-world. Unless these words are used when joking or lying, they are often an extension of the confusion of needs and wants. When someone labels something as awful or terrible, they often equate it with something that they *can't stand* or *need* not have. The statement, "It's *terrible* that I lost my job" tends to produce the same anxiety or anger that the statement, "I *can't stand* that I lost my job" does.

Another Brief Psychology Lesson

In the early 1900's, two researchers, Robert Yerkes and John Dodson (1908) discovered that there is an optimal level of arousal for each task. If a person is not sufficiently physically aroused for the task at hand, his or her performance on it will be poor. Conversely, if a person is too physically aroused for the task at hand, his or her performance will also be poor. Their discovery became known as the Yerkes-Dodson Law.

The optimal level of arousal is different for each task. For example, if a mother's child were trapped under a car, she likely would have a difficult time *calmly* lifting the car off of her child. For her to lift the car successfully, she would need to be sufficiently distressed (aroused). However, if she were too aroused, she might freeze and not be able to approach the car.

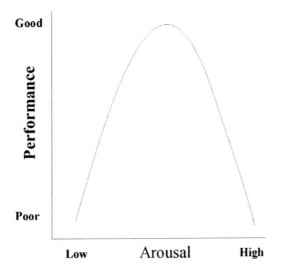

Yerkes and Dodson (1908) discovered that there
is an optimal level of arousal for each task.

Imagine if she were to take this level of arousal into a test-taking situation. She likely would be too aroused for that task, as that level of arousal would make it difficult to think and to remember what she had learned.

The words "awful, horrible, and terrible" tend to create too much arousal. The attitude, "I do not care about this," tends to create insufficient arousal. The word "unfortunate" tends to produce an optimal level of arousal.

Dr. Albert Ellis (1988) has written extensively on the topic of catastrophizing. He emphasizes that nothing is *objectively* awful, horrible, or terrible. For example, many people throughout the world viewed the events of September 11, 2001 in the United States as terrible. However, on that same day, there were people who were dancing in the streets with joy at the site of America being harmed. If the terrorist attacks of September 11 were *objectively* terrible, everyone would have seen them that way.

Since nothing is objectively terrible, horrible, or awful, we are free to label *anything* as such and to make ourselves miserable as a result. We are also free to label *anything* as being "unfortunate" or "inconvenient" and make ourselves feel more along the lines of calm. The question is, "Which way of labeling a personally undesirable event will work better for us?" The word "unfortunate" implies that a situation is personally *undesirable but survivable.*

Keep in mind, though, that nothing is objectively unfortunate either. That's why in Rational Living Therapy we like to add the words, "for me." The statement, "This is an unfortunate situation for me" suggests that this situation is contrary to *my* goals, what *I* want out of life, and I *dislike* that fact."

Labeling a personally undesirable situation as unfortunate does not mean that one does not care about it or is uninterested in correcting the situation. As the Yerkes-Dodson Law demonstrates, labeling these situations as unfortunate places a person in a much better position to correct them than does labeling them terrible, horrible, or awful.

But aren't there some situations that are worse than others?

The answer is "for whom?" This question again implies that there are objectively good, bad, and neutral situations, events, or conditions. However, what is considered good to one person might be considered bad to another, and this is determined primarily by what one's goals are.

Some situations interfere with our own goals more than others, thus making them *"personally worse"* for us. These personally worse situations often require more time, energy, and effort to correct than do other situations. We still are better off labeling these situations as "personally worse" and as "unfortunate for me," instead of labeling them as terrible, horrible, and awful.

(15) Magical Worry

Worry is fearful thinking. It is the act of obsessively thinking about a feared outcome.

How often does what you worry about actually happen? I'll bet that unless you are very selective in worrying, your answer to this question is, "not that often." After years of worrying about things only to have our worries not come true, sometimes we unintentionally make a connection—when we worry about things, they do not happen. This "connection" often leads us to believe that our worrying keeps unwanted events from occurring. We then become afraid *not* to worry. This is what Maxie Maultsby, M.D. calls "magical worry."

Maultsby (1984) calls worry "civilized voodoo" because worry does not keep events from happening, as worry is *only* thinking. Worrisome thoughts cannot influence, change, or prevent a situation. *Actions* prevent situations from occurring, not worrisome thoughts. So if a person *acts* on his or her *concerns*, a better outcome might occur. Simply *worrying* about it will not change anything. Besides giving a person an ulcer, another problem with worry is that it makes it appear as though you are doing something about your situation—"At least I'm worrying about it."

The basic message, therefore, is that refusing it to worry is okay because worry has never protected you. We recommend that you:

(1) Know what you want out of life, like the well-being of yourself and your loved-ones;

(2) If you come across information that shows that your well-being or that of your loved-ones is being threatened, be concerned; and

(3) Act on that concern.

Simply being "concerned" without acting on that concern is not any more helpful than simply worrying.

Sometimes people unintentionally set themselves up for worrying because they are confronted with a situation that seems dangerous, but they approach it anyway. A better approach is to recognize a true threat then act on it.

For example, one January, our son, Aldo, was scheduled to make a trip with several of his classmates and our priest from our home near Pittsburgh, PA to Washington, D.C. I was in Los Angeles during the week preceding his scheduled trip. The day before he was to leave, my wife telephoned me and told me that the weather forecasters were predicting a significant snow storm for the area though which my son would be traveling (a very mountainous area). She wondered if it would be best to keep him home. I asked my wife what the probability of the snow storm was, and she said that the forecasters were estimating an 80% probability.

So I suggested to her, "Honey, we could either allow him to go and worry the entire time, wondering if the bus driver is going to be able to get them to Washington safely, or we could recognize that the chances of Aldo being harmed are significant enough to keep him home." We decided to keep him home.

Since we do not have a crystal ball that tells us what the future will be, we can only make a prediction based on the current facts as best as we can know them. In the situation with our son, the snow storm did occur, and it did in fact become a dangerous situation. Thankfully, the school decided to cancel the trip. Sometimes we err on the side of caution, and in fact the undesired situation does not occur. But until someone invents that crystal ball, we can only base our predictions on the facts that are available to us.

As the saying goes,

> *Worry is like rocking in a rocking chair…*
> *It gives you something to do,*
> *But it gets you nowhere!*

(16) <u>Having Irrational Definitions</u>

Sometimes our definitions of important concepts (like love, respect, trust, caring) can cause us problems in that they can be unrealistic and/or rigid, thus causing us to frustrate ourselves when our goals are not met. Examples of irrational definitions include:

–If a man doesn't spend all of his time with me, he is <u>selfish</u>…

–A person is <u>lazy</u> if she doesn't wash the dishes after she eats…

–If a woman <u>cares</u> about me, she will do this for me every day…

Such definitions are limiting and self-defeating. They can be so limiting that a person ultimately does not get what he or she wants, as in the following example:

<u>Client</u>: "I am a failure."

<u>Me</u>: "Why do you say that?"

<u>Client</u>: "Because my career isn't going as well as I'd like."

Me: "Well, remember that you are not a "failure" but a person who has failed. But I'm interested in knowing what you consider failure to be. What is your definition of the word "failure?"

Client: (Thinks for a moment) "I guess when I don't do things perfectly well."

Me: "And what happens to you when you think of yourself as a failure or that you have failed?"

Client: "I end up giving up!"

Me: "Now look at your definition of failure. What you are saying is that to succeed, you must do something perfectly well. If you do not do something perfectly, you have failed, right?"

Client: "Right."

Me: "And is failing good, bad, or neutral?"

Client: "It's bad!"

Me: "How bad?"

Client: "Very bad!"

Me: "So you see, your definition of "failing" is not going to work in terms of helping you to succeed and to feel good, because it is an all-or-none approach. You believe that a person is either totally successful or totally unsuccessful at something. However, there are degrees of success and failure, as there are various degrees of almost everything. So even if you have done an adequate job at something (enough to achieve a reasonable goal), if it is not perfect, then you have failed, and that's really bad, according to your definition."

Client: "Well, that is how I have thought."

Me: "Okay, then let's replace that thought with something like: I am not a failure, I am a person who sometimes doesn't always achieve perfection at things, and even if I do, the perfection doesn't last for long. That fact only proves one thing—that I am just like everyone else, a Fallible Human Being. However, rarely is something I do a total failure, as there are various aspects of it that I do get right. Anyway, failing is not awful, terrible, or the end-of-the-world, it is only unfortunate! I'll use my disappointment to do reasonably, not perfectly, better."

Pay attention to your definitions of important concepts, particularly those that appear to be causing you trouble. Assess whether or not (or to what degree) your definitions work for you.

(17) Confusing Relying with Depending

To *rely* on someone is to trust they will do something that you *could* do yourself or that you could find other means of doing it. To *depend* on someone is to count on a person to do something that you *cannot* do yourself or find other means of having it done.

Most often, we rely on others because doing so makes life easier. The person who has lost her vision might at first depend on others to guide her around when walking because she does not know how to walk independently. However, when she has learned to walk independently, she might *rely* on others at times to make walking *easier*.

Sometimes we *mistakenly believe* that we are dependent on others because we believe that we do not have the resources to achieve certain goals (such as taking care of ourselves) on our own when in fact we do.

Sometimes people assume that they do not have the potential to be self-reliant because they have not been, at least in certain situations. However, remember the expression, "Just because you haven't doesn't mean you can't."

Being willing to taking a chance to see how well you achieve your goals and care for yourself independently is important. If you are doubting your ability to achieve your goals independently, or to only rely on the help of others, challenge your belief with the Rational Questions. If you continue to have difficulty, discuss this with your therapist.

(18) Confusing Inability with Unwillingness

When a person is *unable* to do something, he or she does not have the skills, knowledge, and/or physical attributes to do it. A person is *unwilling* to do something when he or she has the physical and mental ability to do it, but chooses not to do it, and, instead, chooses a different behavior.

For example, a popular television commercial claimed that "no one can eat just one" of the company's potato chips. The basis of this claim was that the potato chips were so good that once one chip was eaten, one could not help but eat more, as if the chips some how disabled the frontal lobe of the brain causing a person to eat them uncontrollably. What actually happens is:

A	B	C
(Awareness)	(Thought / Belief)	(Emotional Consequence)
Eats a potato chip	"Boy was that good, I think I'll have another one."	Happy Feelings Eats another chip

and this ABC sequence continues until a person either decides to stop eating (stomach is full, jaw muscles hurt, chips no longer tasty, have to go to work) or until he or she runs out of chips! Therefore, it is not that the person *cannot* eat just one, he or she is *unwilling* or *chooses not* to eat just one!

Unwillingness can be the result of different motivators, including fear and desire. A person simply might not have the desire to do something. Other times, however, he or she might feel afraid or very uncomfortable acting in a certain way.

Examples of fear-based unwillingness include:

"I can't tell him 'no.'"

"I couldn't give a speech in front of a large crowd."

"I can't stand the sacrifice it takes to lose weight."

"I can't ask that pretty girl for a date."

"I can't tell the waiter that my steak is not cooked properly."

In each case, a person has the physical and mental ability to do the things he or she claims cannot be done. However, the *unwillingness* to perform these behaviors is due to anxiety or discomfort. This is an important distinction, because in each case a person does *not* need to *learn how* to perform these behaviors—he or she wants to learn how to perform them *comfortably*.

Therefore, if you find yourself believing that you "cannot" do something, ask yourself:

"Do I have the physical and mental ability to do it?"

"If I absolutely had to, would I?"

If you answer "yes" to these questions, what you really mean is that you feel uncomfortable performing the behavior. If so, it is important to rationally dispute the thoughts leading to the discomfort.

(19) <u>Confusing Possibility with Probability</u>

When we plan for the future, we can only make a *prediction* about the outcome because we have no crystal ball to give us absolute certainty. To make a rational prediction, it is important to ask two questions:

Is what I am predicting possible?

If it is possible, what is the probability of it happening?

When a person is anxious, he or she is fears (predicts) that something problematic will happen in the future. To assess this fear, we first ask, "Is it possible for the event to happen?" If it is possible, we then ask, "What is the likelihood of it happening?"

People often assume that if something is *possible*, it must be highly *probable*. This incorrect assumption, or overestimation of the probability of this feared event occurring, often leads to unnecessary concern or anxiety.

For example, I live in the Upper Ohio Valley, which is known for its many bridges. Many residents of this area avoid traveling across those bridges because of a common fear of bridges collapsing while traveling across them. When examining this fear, we first ask, "Is it possible for a bridge to collapse?" Certainly. We know that bridges have collapsed in the past, and there is nothing about any bridge that makes it *absolutely* safe. So this fear is based in reality, and not a bizarre delusion, like being afraid that Martians are controlling your mind. Next we ask, "What is the probability that any given bridge will collapse?" In examining the bridges, we find that they have a very good safety record, with none of them ever coming close to collapsing. We also know that they are inspected regularly, and one was closed for a brief period when an examiner discovered a very minor problem (one that would not have caused the bridge to collapse). Finally, considering the fact that thousands of vehicles travel across these bridges each day with no problem, a *very safe* bet would be that the bridges in my area will remain structurally sound when we travel across them.

Notice that we examine and gather facts when determining possibility and probability. I do not want my clients simply to take my word for it that the bridges are safe. I want them to see what the facts tell us. In examining the actual safety of any given bridge, if we discover that a bridge is not structurally sound, that it has not been maintained, and that a civil engineer suggests avoiding driving across it, I am going to avoid that bridge as well!

When a Low Probability Just Isn't Enough

Sometimes people tell me, "I do not care if God himself were to tell me that the airplane is not going to crash, I still would not get on it!" When this is the case, there are often underlying assumptions (as described in Chapter Four) that make it difficult to benefit from a low probability of an undesirable event occurring.

The following example demonstrates how underlying assumptions make low probability irrelevant to a person.

Client: "I'm afraid of flying."

Me: "Are you afraid of flying, or are you afraid of crashing?"

Client: (Laughing) "I guess I'm afraid of crashing!"

Me: "That's right. First, let's discuss whether it is possible for a plane to crash. Obviously it is, right, because they have. Now, what is the probability that any given plane that you would travel in would crash? Did you know that as we speak there are thousands of airplanes in the air, and this is the case for most of the day, every day?"

Client: "Sure, I know all that. But it wouldn't matter to me if God himself told me that a plane that I wanted to get on would not crash, I still wouldn't get on it."

Me: "Even if God told you that there was 100% certainty that you would make it to your destination safely?"

Client: "Yep."

Me: "Okay. Well, this might sound like a silly question, but besides it ruining your day, if the plane you were on were to crash, what would be the problem, as far as you are concerned, if the plane were to crash and you were to die?"

Client: "That would mean that my kids wouldn't have a father."

Me: "O.k. And as far as you are concerned, what problem would there be if your children did not have a father?"

Client: "They would grow up disturbed."

Me: "And if they grew up disturbed, why would that be a problem, as far as you are concerned?"

Client: "Because they would have a miserable life."

Me: "What would it be like for you if you knew that your children had a miserable life?"

Client: "It would be terrible. I couldn't take that."

As long as the client in this example fears such a negative outcome, he will be unwilling to take even the slightest chance that the feared outcome would occur. By learning how to overcome the fear of his children necessarily growing up disturbed, he will be more willing to take advantage of the excellent safety record of the airline industry.

It is important to note, though, that sometimes people *underestimate* the probability of an event occurring, and develop problems as a result. Veteran professional boxer Tommy Morrison announced in 1996 that he had contracted the HIV virus. At a press conference to announce his retirement from boxing, Morrison commented, "I thought I had a better chance of winning the lottery than of contracting HIV…" While it is not particularly easy to contract HIV through heterosexual sex, the chances of contracting HIV through it are far greater than the chances of winning the lottery. Apparently, his underestimation of the chances of contracting HIV led him to engaging in behaviors that increased the likelihood of contracting it.

Therefore, when making a prediction, first determine if it is possible for the event to occur. If it is possible, next assess the probability of it occurring. If you determine that it is possible, and the probability is high, then determine the severity of the consequence. If I know that there is a high probability that I will get a paper cut while doing paperwork, I might be willing to take that chance. However, if it were very probable that doing paperwork would kill me, I would likely refrain from doing it!

(20) <u>Projection</u>

People often assume that because they have certain beliefs, other people must think the same way. So they assume that the motives of others are similar to their own. For example, someone who views herself as ugly might have the beliefs:

> "This boy is not interested in me because he thinks I'm ugly.
> Why wouldn't he think I'm ugly? It's obvious that I am!"

While it is true that there are very common beliefs in our society, that does not mean that we all think alike. No two people have the same set of wants, likes, dislikes, opinions, values, and morals. Consequently, it is a mistake to assume that others *must* think, feel, and want as you do, because we are all different. Some men like very slender women, while others like those who are "full-figured." Some women like men with beards, and others do not. Our diversity makes it important to realize that people can have opinions that differ from our own. This is particularly true when examining our perception of ourselves. People often view us differently than we view ourselves, especially when our own opinion is very negative.

Sometimes projection occurs when we accuse others of being motivated to do something because we ourselves have that motivation. The husband who often questions the whereabouts of his wife, believing that she is having an affair, might be fearing this because he himself has had an affair. His own motivation to have an affair shapes how he perceives his wife.

<u>Is My Assumption The Result of Projection?</u>

If we....	*We tend to...*
Speak badly of others.....	Think that they speak badly about us.
Cheat others......	Think that they are cheating us.
Have a low opinion of our own attributes....	Assume others dislike our attributes as well.

Since projection is mind-reading, ask yourself, "Is my assumption of what someone is thinking influenced by what *I* tend to think in similar situations?" If so, remind yourself that just because you hold that belief does not mean that others do as well.

(21) <u>Being Upset About an "Idea" Rather than the "Facts"</u>

As is the case with "irrational should statements," people often upset themselves over the *idea* of something rather than the actual consequences of it. In these cases, a person is upset because he or she thinks it is a requirement to be upset, regardless of the actual consequences of the seemingly undesirable situation. The following example illustrates this point.

<u>Client</u>: "I hate how my nose looks!"

<u>Me</u>: "In your opinion, what is wrong with your nose?"

<u>Client</u>: "I hate that it's crooked."

<u>Me</u>: "How has your nose been a problem for you?"

<u>Client</u>: "What do you mean?"

<u>Me</u>: "Are there any goals that you have not achieved because of your nose? Is there anything that you want that do not have because of your nose?"

<u>Client</u>: "I guess not."

<u>Me</u>: "Really think about it for a moment."

<u>Client</u>: (Thinks for a moment) "I can't think of any problems that my nose has created for me."

<u>Me</u>: "So it seems to me that you have been upset about the *idea* that your nose is crooked instead of any consequence of it. What you are saying is that your life is the way you want it to be despite your nose. Your upset has been the result of the idea that a nose shouldn't be crooked, and if it is, you should be upset about it, *regardless of whether or not the nose actually causes you any problems.*"

<u>Client</u>: "I think that I see what you mean."

<u>Me</u>: "Great. I encourage you to apply this logic to anything with which you might be dissatisfied. Ask yourself, 'I am dissatisfied because of a consequence or because of an idea that I should be?'"

Take a moment to think of all of the situations or conditions with which we have been taught that we *should* be upset. Examples include:

**Examples of Situations / Conditions With Which
We Have Been Taught We are "Supposed" to Be Upset**

Being "Too" Short	Parents Not Loving You
Being "Overweight"	Not Having a Romantic Partner
Turning 40-years-old	Losing Your Hair
Having Crooked Teeth	People Thinking Negatively of you

While each of these examples could be practical problems for a person, they are not necessarily. It depends on whether a person has *goals* with which these situations or conditions would interfere. Most of us have learned, though, that these situations/conditions (and many others like them)*necessarily* are problems, that we should be upset with them, and that there is something wrong with us if we are not upset in response to them.

When considering whether you are experiencing a practical problem, ask yourself, "Do I think that the situation at hand is a problem because it is interfering with achieving my goals, or do I think it is a problem simply because I have been taught that it is?"

(22) "Nonsense Arguments"

When we have a goal that we want to achieve or a problem that we want to solve, we are usually more effective in doing so when we are best able to use our physical and mental resources. In other words, the more we are able to focus on the goals, the more we can use our intelligence and physical ability to achieve them. Nonsense arguments distract us from our goals.

Nonsense arguments are those statements people make to themselves or others that can be totally accurate, totally inaccurate, or somewhere in between. However, accuracy of the statement is not the issue. The problem with nonsense arguments is that they distract a person from an important task at hand.

Nonsense arguments often are made in the form of a "historical if" or "if only" statement, such as:

"If only I hadn't had that accident, I would be able to walk today."

"If only my husband hadn't divorced me, I wouldn't have the problems I'm having today."

"If only my parents had worked harder, I'd have a nice inheritance today."

"If only that car hadn't run over my foot, I wouldn't have a broken foot."

These "if only's" are largely irrelevant. The relevant question is, "What do I do about my situation now?" The only reason to spend any amount of time thinking about personally negative events of the past is to learn from them.

As we say in the Pittsburgh, Pennsylvania area, "There is no point in trying to shovel last year's snow. You can't shovel it, but you can't get stuck in it either."

Focus your energy on resolving any current concerns, learning from your past, and creating a happy tomorrow.

(23) Irrational Hopelessness/Helplessness

Hopeless thinking is an example of jumping to conclusions, no matter how much a person has researched the problem about which he or she is thinking hopelessly.

For a person to think hopelessly, he or she must make the following assumption:

"I know all there is to know about this problem.
If I do not see a solution to it, one must not exist!"

Even after a *seemingly* exhaustive search for a solution has been conducted, to think hopelessly, one must *assume* that no solution exists beyond where they have looked, and that no solution *could ever* exist. It is this *assumption* that can lead a person to stop searching and to fail to take advantage of a potential solution.

Why do people jump to such pessimistic conclusions? Various reasons exist, including:

1. Previous learning about what is possible or available

As we grow up, we are taught what is possible and what is not. For many of us, we first believe that *anything* is possible. We then come to "learn" from various sources what *people* can and cannot do, then we learn more specifically what *we* can and cannot do. Sometimes, though, what we learn is not worth learning because it is not accurate.

Sometimes we learn from others teaching us by word or example, or both. Our father's and mother's accomplishments demonstrate to us what is possible. They might also encourage or discourage us with statements like, "You can do it" or "You'll never amount to much," or statements about themselves, like, "I'll never get ahead" or "It's always someone else that's successful, never me."

This learning creates underlying assumptions (refer to Chapter Four) that cause us to assume automatically that we can or cannot successfully accomplish something.

When examining whether or not you have the potential to achieve a goal or to correct a personally undesirable situation, ask yourself, "Is it possible for a human being to do this?" In other words, have other people like you, with the same attributes and background, accomplished what you want to accomplish? A simple "not that I know of" answer will not suffice. I encourage you to do some research to see.

Also realize that just because others have not accomplished what you want to does not necessarily mean it cannot be done. Has anyone ever tried? If so, why were they not successful? What could you do differently?

When people say that something is impossible, I'm often reminded of Coach Doug Blevins. Coach Blevins is the National Football League's most sought after kicking coach. His star pupil is Adam Vinatieri, who won two Super Bowls for the New England Patriots with last-second field goals. Coach Blevins had a dream since he was a child to coach in the NFL. Today, he is an outstanding kicking coach despite the fact that he has never walked a day in his life. He has cerebral palsy and has been confined to a wheelchair since he was a young child. How Coach Blevins managed to (1) learn kicking technique, (2) figure out how to teach, from a wheelchair, athletes how to kick, and (3)convinced professional football teams that he could coach their kickers, is beyond me. How many times do you think he was discouraged from pursuing his dream?

2. Impatience/Low Frustration Tolerance

People sometimes begin thinking hopelessly *because* they have given up.

Sometimes they end their pursuit of a goal because they are impatient, not willing to wait for success. The attitude is, "If I can't have it (or fix it) now, forget it." Impatience is often the result of confusing needing with wanting, as in, "I need to have it now!" It is important to change this attitude to, "I'd rather have it now, but I certainly can wait!"

At other times, low frustration tolerance causes a person to be intolerant of failing. The attitude is, "If success (or a solution) does not come easily, forget it." If a person views road blocks, setbacks, and frustrations along the way to success as terrible, horrible, and awful, he or she will not attempt to achieve anything that requires much effort. It is important to change this attitude to, "I wish that success and solutions would always come to me easily, but I do not need them to." Remember, though, that about the only thing that comes easily to us is trouble. Everything else takes work!

3. Taking Someone's Word for It

As we will discuss in greater detail later in this book, "expert voice" is a significant factor that helps us determine whether we believe something to be a fact. When we believe that someone is an expert, we are likely to view what they tell us as credible, and, therefore, factual. Sometimes, though, the "expert" is not as knowledgeable as we think.

I remember some of my high school teachers "informing" me and my classmates that a person had to be exceptionally intelligent to get accepted into law school and to practice law. They also informed us that a student needed "straight A's" to be accepted into law school. As young, naive high school students, we accepted what they said as being factual. We figured that if our teachers said it, it must be so. My teachers were wrong on both counts. It is hard to tell how many potentially exceptional lawyers they discouraged with their "knowledge."

I encourage you to refuse to take *any* expert's word for it. Experts only know what they know. God only knows what they do not know. Obtain a second and third opinion. Research solutions to your problem or approaches to achieving your goal. As long as your goal or situation is important to you, continue your search. Why not? What do you have to lose? However, what do you have to gain by finding a solution?

I also encourage you, though, to search *rationally*. The irrational pursuit of a goal or solution leads to a person forsaking other goals and important concerns. Keep in mind that hope does not require facts. We "hope" when we do not have facts. When we *know* that there is a solution to our problem, we do not need to hope. So a person is always free to hope that their situation will improve, regardless of the situation!

(24) <u>Too Much/Too Little Problem</u>

People often relate their or other's attributes or behavior to a goal without realizing it. Common examples of this include:

I'm too fat!   I'm too skinny!
I'm too short!   I'm too lazy!
I'm too ugly!   I'm too dumb!
I drink too much!   I eat too much!
He sleeps too much!   She swears too much

A very appropriate and relevant question to ask yourself or others in response to such statements is, "For what?" In other words, "What are you too fat for?" The word "too" in this case is an adverb that suggests "an excessive amount of." Therefore, the word "too" suggests that it is in relation to something. So if I say that I am "too fat," I am implying that I will not be able to achieve a goal as the result of how much fat I have.

If someone weighing 700 pounds were to say to you, "I am too fat," you might agree with him. However, this statement suggests that his size necessarily would keep him from achieving a goal. This underlying assumption often leads people to avoid pursuing a goal. The following example illustrates this point.

<u>Client</u>: (Female in her late thirties who weighed 400 pounds) "I am too fat."

<u>Me</u>: "Too fat for what?"

<u>Client</u>: "I'm not sure what you mean."

<u>Me</u>: "You said that you are too fat. When people say that, they are implying that their size necessarily is a problem for them—that it is keeping them from achieving a goal. So I'm wondering what you are too fat for. How is being your size a problem?"

<u>Client</u>: "I'll never get a boyfriend and get married. Who would want someone this fat?"

<u>Me</u>: "Okay. Well, I won't deny the fact that in our society, the thinner a person is, to a certain point, the more attractive they tend to be seen by more people. With that said, what you are saying is that it is impossible for you to attract a mate and get married because of your size. Now, do you know of anyone who is at least your size that has attracted a mate and has gotten married?"

<u>Client</u>: "Actually, I know of three women who are at least my size that are married."

<u>Me</u>: "Okay. Well, if you are, using your words, too fat to get married, why were they not too fat? How did these women manage to meet their husbands and get married?"

<u>Client</u>: "They all three met their husbands at social events."

<u>Me</u>: "Do you go to social events or gatherings?"

<u>Client</u>: "No. I go to work then spend the rest of the evening at home with my parents."

Me: "So one possible explanation as to why you are not married like they are is that you have not placed yourself in a position for men to get to know you. Your assumption that they necessarily would not like you because of your size has kept you away from them."

Client: "I think that I see what you mean."

Me: "Now, I'm not suggesting that you not work at losing weight if that is what you are wanting to do. It probably would increase your chances of attracting a mate. We just disputed the assumption that you *have to* lose weight to attract a mate."

This mental mistake is related to the mistake of "being upset about the idea of something rather than one's reality." Many people believe that being 400 pounds *itself* is a problem, and thus the statement, "I'm too fat."

Remember that we discussed the concept of a "practical problem" earlier in this book. A practical problem is the result of something standing in the way of our achieving a goal. Therefore, one must have a goal to have a practical problem. If being 400 pounds is a practical problem, the question "for what?" helps us to determine the goal that being that size might affect, and then to decide whether it actually does present an obstacle to achieving that goal.

I encourage you to challenge any underlying assumptions that you might have that the phrases "too much" or "not enough" suggest by first asking, "for what?"

(25) Ambivalent Beliefs

Ambivalent beliefs are beliefs that a person believes just strongly enough to feel bad about *not* acting on them, but not strongly enough *to* act on them. They are usually moralistic, but need not be.

Many people have an ambivalent belief regarding premarital sex. They believe that premarital sex is wrong. However, they believe that it is wrong just strongly enough to feel guilty after having premarital sex, but not strongly enough to keep themselves from having it. This "being on the fence" approach does not work. It sets a person up for failure.

This is one of those rare situations when I suggest all-or-none thinking. Either think that premarital sex is wrong, and, therefore, learn how to stop having it, or give up the belief and have it. Of course, it is important for a person also to consider whether (in this example) premarital sex is *rational*, independent of whether or not it is "wrong."

If you do things repeatedly that you later regret, you might have ambivalent beliefs associated with those behaviors. If so, discover what those beliefs are and then apply the rational question to them. Relate those beliefs to your goals and determine how important it is either to act on them or give them up.

(26) Correlation Equals Causation

When two things occur at the same time (correlation), sometimes people assume that one thing caused the other (causation). For example, before learning the Emotional ABC's, you might have come to the conclusion at times that if someone said something to you and you were upset in response, that meant that what the person said caused you to be upset. It *seemed* that way because what they said and how you felt happened at virtually the same time.

Just because two things occur concurrently does not mean that one causes the other. For example:

If "A" and "B" happen at the same time:

"A" could have caused "B"

"B" could have caused "A"

"C" could have caused both "A" and "B"

Did you know that there is a positive correlation between intelligence, knowledge, and height, so that the taller a person is, the more intelligent and knowledgeable he or she tends to be? Does this mean that being tall *causes* a person to be more intelligent and knowledgeable, or does it mean that being more intelligent and knowledgeable *causes* a person to be taller? Actually, there is a third variable to consider. The fact is, we begin life shorter and grow taller as we age. We also begin life less intelligent and knowledgeable and grow more so as we age. Therefore, as we age, we grow taller and become more intelligent and knowledgeable.

An example of the "correlation equals causation" mental mistake is "magical worry," which was discussed earlier in this chapter. Remember that with magical worry, people notice that usually after they worry, the undesirable outcome does not occur. After a while, the causal relationship is established, "If I worry about it, it won't happen." What is not realized is that a third factor caused the event *not* to happen. Another example of the "correlation equals causation" mental mistake is the mental mistake of "personalization and blame." If a person has a stroke after being upset in reaction to something I say, it would *seem* as though (1) I caused his distressed feelings, (2) the upset feelings caused his stroke, and therefore, (3) I caused his stroke.

One way to avoid making this mental mistake is to become knowledgeable of the subject matter at hand. Do some research into the subject. Ask questions, like, "What are other possible explanations?"

Concluding Remarks About the Common Mental Mistakes

I encourage you to become very familiar with the common mental mistakes so that you can recognize if you make them. These mental mistakes have become for me what some singing on the Fox television show, *American Idol*, is to my wife (we love that show, by the way). My wife has a degree in music education, and she specialized in voice. When she hears someone sing off key (as they often do on *American Idol*) it hurts her ears. When I hear shoulds, musts, and have-to's, it hurts my ears! That's exactly what we want for these mistakes to be for us—noise.

Common Emotional Problems and the Common Mental Mistakes

While any of the Common Mental Mistakes can lead to the following feelings, those listed with each emotion are the most common culprits.

<u>Anger</u>
  Irrational Should Statements (Directed Outward)
  Confusing Needs with Wants
  Can't Stand-itis
  Catastrophizing
  Blame
  Confusing "Choosing to" with "Having to" / "Force" with "Choice"

<u>Guilt</u>
  Irrational Should Statements (Directed Inward)
  Confusing Needs with Wants
  Catastrophizing
  Personalization

<u>Depression</u>
  Irrational Hopelessness / Helplessness
  Confusing Needs with Wants
  Catastrophizing

<u>Anxiety</u>
  Confusing Needs with Wants
  Confusing Possibility with Probability
  Magical Worry
  Can't Stand-itis
  Catastrophizing

Mid-Therapy Assessment

Please complete the following questionnaire honestly. This will help you and your therapist assess what you are experiencing, how you are thinking, and how you are feeling.

Circle the answer that best represents your situation.

	Strongly Disagree	Disagree	Neutral	Agree	Strongly Agree
1. Things in my life are different than they should be.	1	2	3	4	5
2. People make me upset.	1	2	3	4	5
3. I can't stand certain things in my life.	1	2	3	4	5
4. I need to think well of myself before I can do certain things.	1	2	3	4	5
5. There are things in my life that are simply awful and terrible.	1	2	3	4	5
6. How I feel depends on how people treat me.	1	2	3	4	5
7. Certain situations make me upset.	1	2	3	4	5
8. People can't feel and act better until their situation changes.	1	2	3	4	5
9. You can't trust someone again after they have violated your trust.	1	2	3	4	5
10. People need to be concerned about other peoples' opinions.	1	2	3	4	5
11. I have a right to be upset.	1	2	3	4	5
12. There isn't much hope for me to feel or act differently because I have tried before and failed. That means I can't.	1	2	3	4	5
13. It's important for me to focus on how I feel and what I do as the main indicators of how well I am doing in therapy.	1	2	3	4	5

Mid-Therapy Assessment

Please complete the following questionnaire honestly. This will help you and your therapist assess what you are experiencing, how you are thinking, and how you are feeling.

Circle the answer that best represents your situation.

	Strongly Disagree	Disagree	Neutral	Agree	Strongly Agree
14. If I don't see it, it doesn't exist.	1	2	3	4	5
15. I just can't cope with things.	1	2	3	4	5
16. I need medication to make me feel better.	1	2	3	4	5
17. I believe that if I just get things off of my chest, I will feel much better.	1	2	3	4	5
18. If I do something good, I should be rewarded.	1	2	3	4	5
19. If I treat people well, they should treat me well, too.	1	2	3	4	5
20. If I am the only one thinking a certain way, then I must be wrong.	1	2	3	4	5
21. If it feels wrong, it must be wrong.	1	2	3	4	5
22. If it feels right, it must be right.	1	2	3	4	5
23. It's important for a person to follow his or her gut instinct.	1	2	3	4	5
24. If I do something wrong, I should punish myself for it.	1	2	3	4	5

8

The Rational Action Planner

"Putting it All Together"

The Rational Action Planner (RAP) is a technique that I developed that brings together what you have learned so far into a single procedure that enables you to develop a plan of action that is more consistent with your goals.

The RAP technique is performed on a two-sided prepared form (see below), or it can be done on a blank sheet of paper by copying the sections of the form.

The first side of the RAP form includes the old or current ABC's of the situation, including thoughts and unwanted/problematic feelings and behaviors. It also includes a section to place your goals for the situation, a Camera Check section for the description you gave in the "A" section, and a section to record which thoughts pass the Rational Questions.

The second side of the RAP form is where you develop your *new* ABC's for the situation, including a camera-checked "A" section, new rational beliefs, and the desired emotional/behavioral response (how you want to act and feel in the situation). It is the information on this side of the form that you will want to practice using the various techniques described in the following chapters.

The following is an example of a properly completed Rational Action Planner. Use it as a guide for your RAP's. Refuse to concern yourself with completing the RAP correctly the first couple of tries. Instead, do your best and get feedback from your therapist. Notice that the **first step** is to write down that of which you were aware or to which you were reacting (the "A" in the ABC's of Emotions). The **second step** is to write down your beliefs about it (the "B" in the ABC's). You might have one thought or one-hundred thoughts. If you have more thoughts than the space provided allows, write the remaining thoughts on another sheet of paper. The **third step** is to write down how you felt and what you did (the "C" in the ABC's). The **fourth step** is to record what your goals were in that situation, either goals that you were aware of at the time (conscious goals) or those that you probably had in that situation (implied goals). The **fifth step** is to do a Camera Check of what you wrote in the "A" section and to record what a camera would actually show. The **sixth step** is to apply the Rational Questions to each thought that you listed in the "B" section. Write down whether or not a thought is rational under each thought in the "B" section. If any of the thoughts are irrational, you will need to complete the next side of the RAP, the "New ABC's."

Rational Action Planner™

Old ABC's

A (What you are aware of)	**B** (Thoughts or Beliefs about it)	**C** (Emotional & Physical Reaction)
My girlfriend told me that she wants to break up with me, and I fell all to pieces.	*1. I need her because I'm nothing without her! (Irrational)* *2. It's terrible that she wants to break up with me. (Irrational)* *3. I'll never be happy again, and that's terrible! (Irrational)*	*Very nervous* *Begged her to not break up with me* *Told her that I'd kill myself if she broke up with me*

What were (are) your goals in this situation (Conscious or Implied)?

	Achieved?
1. *Remain calm*	*No*
2. *Tell her what I really meant*	*No*
3. *Do things to encourage her to stay*	*No*
4.	

Camera Check of "A" Section (What Would a Camera Show)	**Rational Questions**
It would show her telling me that she wanted to break up with me, but it would not show me falling to pieces, like a pile of body parts!	Apply the Rational Questions To Each of the Thoughts in the "B" Column and Write Down Whether or Not They Passed Them. 1. Is my thinking based on Fact? 2. Does my thinking help me achieve my goals? 3. Does my thinking help me feel the way I want to feel? **Keep any thoughts that pass the Rational Questions and replace any that do not.**

Rational Action Planner™
Side 2

New ABC's

<u>A</u>	<u>B</u>	<u>C</u>
(Camera Checked)	(New Thoughts to Practice)	As a result of my new thinking, I'll feel and do this:

Whenever I'm in this Situation:

I'm around her, think of her, or see her

I'll think this:

Anything that is physically present is "something." Therefore, it is impossible for me to be a "nothing." What I am is a human being. I need no one or nothing for me to be a human being. I was born with the same human worth as everyone else, and no one or nothing can take that away from anyone!

I didn't need my ex-girlfriend—I only wanted her. Therefore, I'll feel appropriately sad as I think of losing her as a disappointment, not something that is terrible or that I can't stand. Certainly I can stand her breaking up with me, because I am!

The sooner I calmly accept the fact that we ended this relationship, the sooner I will find happiness in another relationship or with something else.

Feel calm

Treat her kindly

Do these new thoughts pass the Rational Questions?

Practice imagining yourself in the "A" Section, Thinking the "B" Section, and Reacting like the "C" Section. Act "As If" you believe the new thoughts until they feel comfortable to you.

How do we produce the new thoughts in the "B" column of the new ABC's? We base the new thoughts on the reasons the old thoughts were irrational. The new rational replacement thoughts are a response or rebuttal to the old irrational thoughts. **Apply the Rational Questions to those new thoughts to make certain that they are in fact rational.**

What do I do now that I have completed the RAP?

After completing the new ABC's, **read aloud the thoughts in the "B" column** at least once every day for one month. Why read the new thoughts aloud? Reading them aloud uses two senses, visual and auditory. Some people are better at remembering something that they have heard than something that they have seen or read. So reading the new thoughts aloud makes it more likely that you will remember them.

Also, **practice imagining** yourself in the situation you described in the new "A" section, while thinking the new thoughts in the "B" section and feeling and acting like the "C" section. Practice this visualization at least once every day for one month.

Finally, **begin acting "as if"** you believe what you wrote in the new "B" column by acting out your "C" column whenever you are in the "A" situation. As you will see in the next chapter, practicing your new thoughts, feelings, and behaviors is very important.

The following is a blank Rational Action Planner. Feel free to copy it for your personal use so that you can use it as often as you wish.

Rational Action Planner™

Old ABC's

A (What you are aware of)	B (Thoughts or Beliefs about it)	C (Emotional & Physical Reaction)

What were (are) your goals in this situation (Conscious or Implied)?

Achieved?

Camera Check of "A" Section (What Would a Camera Show)	Rational Questions
	Apply the Rational Questions To Each of the Thoughts in the "B" Column and Write Down Whether or Not They Passed Them.
	1. Is my thinking based on Fact?
	2. Does my thinking help me achieve my goals?
	3. Does my thinking help me feel the way I want to feel?
	Keep any thoughts that pass the **Rational Questions** and replace any that do not.

Rational Action Planner™
Side 2

New ABC's

<u>A</u>	<u>B</u>	<u>C</u>
(Camera Checked)	(New Thoughts to Practice)	*As a result of my new thinking, I'll feel and do this:*
Whenever I'm in this Situation:	*I'll think this:*	

Do these new thoughts pass the Rational Questions?

Practice imagining yourself in the "A" Section, Thinking the "B" Section, and Reacting like the "C" Section. Act "As If" you believe the new thoughts until they feel comfortable to you.

9

The Importance of Practice

Every day, people intentionally practice in one form or another. They may go to basketball practice, dance practice, band practice, or play rehearsal. School children practice the "fire drill," their multiplication tables, and their ABC's. Police officers practice firing their guns. I could go on all day!

Why do we practice, and why is it important? It is often said that "practice makes perfect." Well, almost so, anyway. Practice helps us in three ways:

(1) it helps us learn the proper way of performing a behavior,
(2) it helps feel comfortable with a behavior, and
(3) it helps to make a behavior more automatic.

For example, if I were to ask you to take a pen or pencil, place it in your non-preferred hand, and write with that hand for the next month, you would likely experience three things:

(1) Your handwriting would not be as good as it is with the preferred hand;
(2) Writing with the opposite hand would seem strange and wrong to you because you are accustomed to writing with your preferred hand; and
(3) You likely would forget sometimes and begin writing with your preferred hand until you "caught yourself."

The only remedy for these three problems is practice, practice, and more practice! The more you would practice writing with the opposite hand (and refused to write with the preferred hand), the better your penmanship would be, the more comfortable it would feel to you, and the more automatic it would become.

When you first learned to write, it did not feel "funny or wrong" because you were not accustomed to writing a different way. So you had no previous writing experience interfering with learning how to write. You did not have to *un*learn an old way. For emotional change, we are usually in a position to unlearn an already established way of thinking and behaving and to replace it with a new way. This process is what Maultsby (1984) calls "emotional re-education." In other words, we must reeducate ourselves if we are to react differently.

The **stages of emotional re-education** (which are adapted from Maultsby), are:

Stages of Emotional Re-Education

(1) **Intellectual Insight**
(2) **Practice** (Mental and Physical)
    Cognitive-Emotive Dissonance Experienced
(3) **Emotional Insight**
(4) **Personality / Trait Formation** (Habit)

Let's use as an example a person who believes that she is unintelligent. Her belief is, "I am dumb. There is no one dumber than I am." After giving her an intelligence test, we discover that her IQ is 135 (the average is 100). She is very bright. We then point out the many things she has accomplished in her life that are a reflection of her high IQ. Next, **we develop a thought** for her to practice (read aloud to herself every day) that is something like:

"I now have objective evidence that my intellectual level actually is above average. And I now also realize that many things that I have accomplished in my life are the result of my intelligence, not luck. I'm not used to thinking of myself as bright, but the more I practice this thought, the sooner it will feel right to me."

Next, we **ask her to practice this thought** every day by reading it aloud and by visualizing herself accomplishing things she had previously thought were impossible for her to accomplish. We also ask her to begin acting "as if" she believes these new thoughts by actually pursuing her goals, therefore acting as if she is intelligent. As she practices her thought and visualizes herself accomplishing her goals, she tells us that doing so **feels strange and wrong** to her. If she were to "think with her gut," she would say to herself, "Because this new thought feels wrong, it must be wrong." This gut thinking would lead her to abandon the thought. Let's say, though, that she thinks with her head and not her gut and decides to practice the new thought. After a couple of weeks, she tells us that it is beginning to **"feel right" to her.** After a couple of months, she tells us that thinking of herself as intelligent is becoming **automatic** to her.

The first stage of emotional re-education is **Intellectual Insight.** It is achieved when a person understands the effective way, better way, or appropriate way to accomplish something. In the preceding example, she achieves intellectual insight when she realizes that the new thought that we developed for her is an accurate and rational way for her to think.

The second stage of emotional re-education is **Practice.** Practice refers to the actual mental and physical rehearsal of the new behavior. In the preceding example, the mental practice would be her reciting the thought and practicing her visualization daily. Physical practice would come from her working at achieving those goals that require an intellectual level that she thought that did not have. As she practices her new belief, she experiences **cognitive-emotive dissonance.** You might remember from Chapter Two that cognitive-emotive dissonance is that strange, "funny" feeling of wrongness that occurs every time we do, think, or feel something that is the opposite to which we are accustomed. Because it *feels* wrong, it gives us the impression that it *is* wrong. Cognitive-emotive dissonance is normal and unavoidable. It feels wrong for her to think of herself as intelligent because she is accustomed to thinking of herself as "dumb."

After enough practice (usually about one month's worth) she will move to the third stage of emotional re-education—**Emotional Insight.** Emotional insight means that not only does she know "in her head" that the new thought is correct, but now it also "feels right" to her.

With enough practice, she will proceed to the final state of emotional re-education **Personality/Trait Formation.** Personality/trait formation simply means that she has developed a habit. Now she is likely to think automatically of herself as intelligent and capable of achieving her goals.

So What do these Stages of Emotional Re-Education Have to do with Me?

Understanding the stages of emotional re-education helps you to realize (1) **the importance of practice,** (2) **the fact that cognitive-emotive dissonance is normal and to be expected,** and (3) **that they can serve as a guide for where you are in the process of changing.**

Practice is important for two reasons. First, it helps to remove cognitive-emotive dissonance, thus making new thoughts, feelings, and behaviors "feel right." Second, practice helps make the new thoughts and reactions automatic and "there for us" when we need them. So it is incorrect to believe that we can think a new thought just once and expect it to be there for us when we need it.

For example, my son and I participated in a martial art called "Bando." Our Bando instructor regularly implored us to practice our kicks and punches between lessons. If we were to spend only four hours per week (two, two-hour lessons) practicing them, it is likely that the kicks and punches would not be automatic enough for us if attacked. If we had to think about what our instructor taught us to do when attacked *as we are being attacked*, we'd likely get hurt. We want our new thoughts, feelings, and behaviors to be automatic as well.

As was mentioned in Chapter Two, it is important to understand that cognitive-emotive dissonance is normal and to be expected. This understanding helps people to avoid thinking with their gut—it helps people to give what they are practicing a chance, instead of giving up on it because it feels wrong.

Finally, your understanding the stages of emotional re-education now helps you to realize where you are in the process of change for any thought, feeling, or behavior.

How do we change our thoughts, feelings, and behaviors?

To produce long-lasting cognitive, emotional, and behavioral change, a person must:

How to Change Our Thoughts, Feelings, and Behaviors

(1) Realize that the old way of thinking, feeling, or behaving is irrational or otherwise not appropriate;

(2) Develop a new, rational replacement thought;

(3) Refuse to think, feel, or behave the old way;

(4) Practice the new way of thinking, feeling, and behaving;

(5) Tolerate the cognitive-emotive dissonance felt while practicing;

(6) Continue practicing the new thought, feeling, or behavior until it becomes automatic.

Step One, or realizing that the old way of thinking, feeling, or behaving is irrational, is achieved by applying the Rational Questions to the thoughts, feelings, or behaviors. Understanding why the thought is irrational is important because this understanding will help motivate you to avoid thinking that way.

Step Two, or develop a new, rational replacement thought, is achieved by examining the reasons the old thoughts were irrational and basing the new thought on those reasons. Your therapist likely will help you with this step until you get the hang of it.

Step Three, or refusing to think, feel, or behave the old way, is not as difficult as it might seem, particularly if you have done a good job with Step One. Refuse to think in the old terms, and if you happen to find yourself doing so, tell yourself, "*STOP! I refuse to think this way any longer.*" Then recite your new, rational thought to yourself.

Step Four, or practicing the new thoughts, feelings, and behaviors, is done both mentally and physically as was mentioned earlier. Specific practicing techniques are discussed below.

Step Five, or tolerating cognitive-emotive dissonance, involves refusing to take the "funny" or "wrong" feelings as proof that the new way of thinking and behaving is wrong. Additionally, while cognitive-emotive dissonance is not terrible or awful, it can be somewhat uncomfortable. But anything worth achieving takes work and a willingness to tolerate discomfort.

Step Six, or continued practice to make the thought, feeling, or behavior automatic, is important to produce long-term change.

Practicing Techniques

The following are some very effective practicing techniques. Your therapist likely will encourage you to utilize the various techniques. Practice the techniques he or she prescribes for you every day for at least one month.

(1) <u>Mental Practice</u>

1. <u>Simple Script Rehearsal</u> involves writing out a new, rational thought to replace the problem thought and *reading* it at least once a day. *Memorizing* the script is even better, as long as you pay attention to what you are saying to yourself when you recite the thought. Another good way to rehearse the script is to record it on audio tape and listen to it at least once a day.

Associate your thought rehearsal with different behaviors, like brushing your teeth, driving to work, preparing dinner, going to bed, and other behaviors you do routinely. This helps you to *remember* to practice your new belief.

One way to develop your new thought is to utilize the Rational Action Planner as discussed earlier.

The following are generic scripts to combat depression, anger, anxiety, and guilt. They will give you an excellent framework for developing your own unique rational thoughts. Feel free to adapt them to your situation.

A Script to Rid Yourself of Depression

I now realize that my thoughts cause my feelings and behaviors. Thank goodness! I now also realize that depressed feelings are the result of thinking that you absolutely need something, like you can't live without it, and thinking that you'll never get it. I now understand that the only things I really need are those things that keep me alive—air, food, water, etc.…. Everything else is a want or desire. I am entitled to my wants and desires. I just do not need them.

Depression is also the result of thinking hopelessly. Fact is, hopelessness is irrational because it assumes that a person knows all there is to know about his or her problem. No one knows all there is to know about anything!

Since I do want certain things in my life, I'll first remind myself that they are only wants. Then I'll remind myself that no matter how doubtful I might be that I'll be able to obtain those things, it makes no rational sense to assume there is no way to obtain them. Because I want these things, I'll continue to look for ways to obtain them.

I'll remind myself that "just because you haven't doesn't mean you can't…it only means you haven't!" This philosophy will help me to continue searching for a solution.

It's easy to be affected by mental filter—to pay attention only to information that supports hopeless thinking. That's why I'll seek advice from people who know how to correct the problems that I have or achieve the goals I want to achieve.

Ultimately, if I never obtain what I want out of life, that would be unfortunate for me, not terrible, horrible, or awful because they are only wants, not needs. Therefore, since they are wants, I might feel sad or be disappointed—that's it. The human brain does not care what we make ourselves happy with, sad with, or calm with. It truly does not care. So I can be happy with other things if what I have wanted doesn't work out.

Feeling depressed serves no useful purpose, and, in fact, makes a person's situation worse. Therefore, I refuse to make myself depressed. Instead, I'll focus my energy on finding a solution to my problems or a way to achieve my goals.

A Script to Rid Yourself of Anger

Everything is exactly as it should be at any given moment, although it might not be the way I want it to be. My mere wishes, desires, shoulds, and beliefs in right-and-wrong do not make situations magically go my way. Only behaviors influence my environment. If all it took for things to go my way was for me to want it or insist on it, I would have everything I want. My calm acceptance of that fact helps me to make my situations more the way I want them to be.

If a situation is different than I want it to be, I'll remind myself that obviously that means that all the necessary ingredients for it to be that way are present. That will open my mind to determine what those necessary ingredients are and to see what I can do to correct them.

Whenever people anger themselves intensely, they usually think that they can't stand what is going on—that they need their situation to be different than it is. Fact is, the only things I can't stand are those things that could kill me. Everything else I can tolerate. The only things I absolutely need are those things that keep me alive. Everything else is a want.

I'm more likely to get what I want by treating others kindly and approaching them in a calm manner. I can rationally assert myself without being angry or hostile.

I'll do what I can to change those aspects of my life that I want to change. But some things are either unchangeable or very difficult to change (and maybe not worth the effort). Therefore, in those cases, I will view them simply as unfortunate circumstances and/or inconveniences.

Remember that anger is like urinating in your pants—everyone can see it, but you are the only one that can feel it!

A Script to Get Rid Yourself of Anxiety/Worry

It is important for a person to be apprehensive if he or she is in danger—to be afraid enough to take action. However, recognizing a true threat is important. Sometimes it seems that we are in danger when in fact we are not. If I happen to be afraid of something, I'll look at whether what I'm afraid of is possible. If it is, then I'll look at how probable it is. Then I'll look at how well I'd actually be able to cope with the situation if it were to occur, being careful to avoid underestimating my abilities with "can't stand-its" and confusing needing with wanting. The fact is, the only things I cannot stand are those things that could kill me. Everything else is an inconvenience, maybe a very large inconvenience, but still only an inconvenience for me.

I refuse to equate anything with a life-or-death situation when it is not. I now know that worrying is like rocking in a rocking chair—it gave me something to do, but got me nowhere! Worrying itself has never changed anything. Worrying really is civilized voodoo! Worrying about something never magically influenced my environment. If my well-being or the well-being of my loved-ones is threatened, I will be concerned, and then I'll act on that concern. There would be no point in even being concerned if I were unwilling to act on that concern.

I refuse to make myself anxious because I do not like feeling that way. I can stand feeling anxious or nervous, I just do not like it. Feeling anxious is only uncomfortable and inconvenient, not unbearable.

Fact is, I have always handled everything that has ever come my way. The best proof of that is that I am alive. I might not always determine a solution for a problem right away, but I'll figure one out eventually. I'll continue to handle everything that comes my way one way or another.

A Script to Rid Yourself of Guilt

Guilt is anger turned inward. If I happen to guilt myself, I will first look at the facts to determine how much responsibility I actually have for what happened. There is no point in blaming myself if it is not my fault. There also is no point in blaming myself more than the degree to which I actually am responsible.

If I am at fault in any way, I'll remind myself that I should have done exactly what I did because I did everything necessary to do it. That does not mean that I think that it was right or good for me to do it. It only means that one plus one equals two, no matter how much I want it to equal four. All of the necessary ingredients for me to do it were present, or I would not have done it. So if I want to avoid repeating such mistakes, I'll seek to discover what those necessary ingredients are and work at changing them.

Fact is, I could spend the rest of my life making myself miserable about what happened, but that will not in any way make up for anything, or keep it from happening in the future. What keeps me from repeating problem behaviors is actively choosing to do something different, and I don't have to feel guilty to do that!

It's also important for me to assess accurately what happened and what I did. Did I violate some arbitrary rule? I remind myself that people make up all sorts of rules that have no scientific backing to them and then act like the world is going to fall apart if someone breaks one of those rules. I now realize that I am a fallible human being just like everyone else. People make mistakes!

The bottom line is that guilt is a useless emotion that did nothing but made me feel bad. If I want to change my behavior, I'll learn how, and do it! I cannot erase history! I can make it more likely that I'll have a happy future by refusing to dwell on the past.

(2) <u>Rational Visualization</u> involves practicing mental imagery of your desired outcomes. It is rehearsing by visualizing how you want to act and feel.

Rational Living Therapists are very motivated to encourage their client to utilize rational visualization because it works. Why does it work? Because the human brain does not know the difference between an image produced from external stimuli and an image produced internally. That's why dreams are so real to us—why we wake up from a nightmare with our heart pounding. When we have a nightmare (or any other dream), as far as our brain is concerned, we are actually experiencing what we are dreaming. If our brain knew the difference, that we are not actually experiencing what we are dreaming, we would not have the physical and emotional response to the dream that we do.

Rational Visualization Instructions

A. Develop a new rational thought to practice.

B. Have a clear idea how you want to feel and act in the relevant situation.

C. Place your self in a comfortable position and practice a relaxation technique. My tape, "Rational Progressive Relaxation," provides a way to learn to relax quickly and deeply. I recommend that you either purchase this tape (by calling 1-800-853-1135) or have your therapist teach you progressive relaxation as a very effective method of relaxing.

D. After you have relaxed yourself to a personally desirable level, practice visualizing your new behaviors/reactions. Imagine yourself thinking your new thoughts in those relevant situations. If by chance you start to feel anxious or uncomfortable in any way while practicing your visualization (sometimes the case if when a person works at overcoming a fear), stop the visualization, relax yourself again, and resume the visualization. If you repeatedly feel anxious or uncomfortable, suspend the visualization and discuss your experience with your therapist. There might be additional distressing thoughts that have not yet been addressed.

Rational visualization can help you move beyond a sticking point. For example, if a person were concerned that she will die of heart disease in her 50's because many people in her family have, I would have her practice visualizing herself as a very healthy, vibrant 80-year-old who takes great care of her body, especially her heart.

By the way, many people practice *irrational* visualization. They unintentionally practice their undesired behaviors and reactions by imagining them. The person worried that she will die in her 50's might actually visualize herself dying at that age. Rational Living Therapists teach their clients that we go in the direction that we look. So if we are looking to die in our 50's, we might unintentionally create that reality. If we look to live to be 80-years-old, we are more likely to do what is necessary to create that reality.

3. <u>Self-Hypnosis</u> is another excellent mental practicing technique which is similar to visualization. See Chapter Ten for more details.

4. <u>"Covert" Systematic Desensitization</u> involves breaking a feared situation down into parts to develop an ordered list from the least feared aspect of the situation to the most feared. For example, if a person were afraid of dogs, the following hierarchy would be developed:

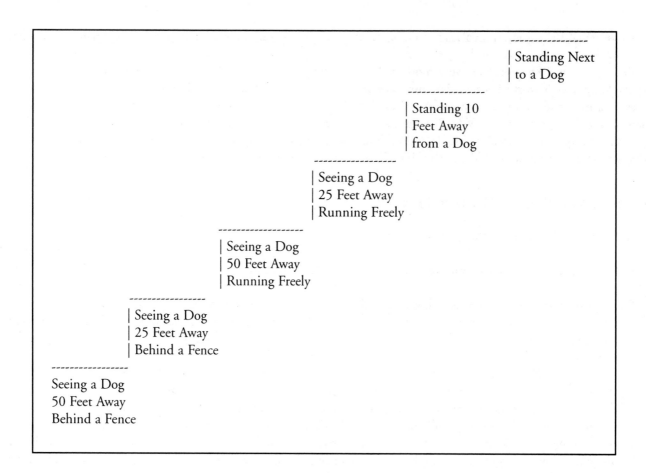

In Covert Systematic Desensitization, we first break down the feared event into steps, and then create an ordered list, or "hierarchy" from least feared to most feared. Relaxation is paired with visualizing each step. The client does not move on to visualizing the next step until he or she is comfortable visualizing the current step.

In this example, the person would begin imagining himself being fifty feet away from a dog that is behind a fence. As the person imagines this, he would keep calm through progressive relaxation as with the rational visualization described earlier. When the person feels comfortable imagining this scene, he then would move to the next most feared aspect, which in this case would we seeing a dog twenty-five feet away behind a fence. He would *not* move to the next level until he felt comfortable with imagining the current level. Once a person feels comfortable with imagining the highest, most feared level, he or she is then ready to begin "in-vivo" systematic desensitization, which is discussed below.

(2) <u>Physical Practice</u>

While mental practice is an excellent way to help you learn new reactions and behaviors, being physically able to perform the action you desire is what your ultimate goal will be for most situations. Sufficient "mental practice" will enable you to perform your desired behaviors *comfortably*. As a result, the next step is to begin regular physical practice of your desired behavior by acting on what you mentally rehearsed. If your problem was feeling anxious while giving speeches, begin to give speeches. If your problem was making yourself angry in reaction to your mother-in-law's comments, begin visiting her while thinking and acting out your new, mentally rehearsed desired thoughts and behaviors.

Sometimes people suffer from "From Missouri-itis," which means that they refuse to believe something until they actually see it. In these cases, a person might continue to feel uncomfortable when physically practicing the new behavior or reaction. If you find that there continues to be some uncomfortableness, you could begin using "In-Vivo" Systematic Desensitization, which is actually physically practicing the desired behavior in successive steps, as in "covert" systematic desensitization described above. Therefore, you physically act out the same steps that you mentally rehearsed until each step feels comfortable to you.

A Willingness to Act "As If"

A willingness to act "as if" is extremely important in emotional and behavioral change. Every time we engage in a new behavior we are acting as if it is something that we do.

For example, I recently hung a new door in my home that was not already "pre-hung." I had experience with installing pre-hung doors, but I had never installed one that was not pre-hung. To install this door, I had to install the hinges myself, trim the side of the door to fit the opening, and make certain that the door was level. After installing the door, my wife said to me, "I am glad that you know how to do these things." I chuckled because I had an *idea* of how to do it, but I had never *actually* done it to know that my understanding of how to was correct. So I faked it! But I did not fake it to deceive people. I faked it for the purpose of practicing. I acted "as if" I knew what I was doing, and I acted "as if" well enough to do a pretty good job. If I had to wait until I knew with absolute certainty that I could install the door well, I would never install it. If someone were to look at the door, they probably would be surprised that this was the first time I had installed a door in this manner.

One way to act "as if" is to pick a role model—someone who is good at what you are wanting to do or who has the attributes that you wish to develop. For a young man wanting to be more comfortable and effective at asking girls for a date, I would encourage him to select a role model—someone who is confident and effective at asking girls for a date. Next, I would ask the young man to study that person, learning how he approaches girls—what he says and does. Then, as the young man approaches women, he would become the person he picked, acting just as he does.

A willingness to act "as if" also can be helpful in getting through personally difficult

situations. If you wake up in the morning not feeling well, and you know that you have a long day ahead of you at work or school, *acting as if* you feel wonderful will help you to get through the day much better than *acting as if* you have never felt worse would. The more you act as if you feel happy, the happier you will feel. Even if you do not believe you have a single reason to be happy, *acting as if* you are happy will make it more likely that you will find reasons to be.

What Makes a New Thought "Grow?"

As I'm sure you have discovered by now, the most important aspect of "getting better" is to change your thinking. If we liken a new, rational thought to a seed that we are planting, we want to water this seed, give the seedling plenty of fertilizer, and nurture it until it becomes a full-grown, healthy plant.

There are four factors that will make your new thought grow. We are going to use these four factors that are like fertilizer for your new, rational thoughts.

Desirability of a thought means that a person can see that there are advantages to thinking a thought, even if he or she does not currently believe it. This occurs often in counseling and psychotherapy. The client does not believe a word of what the therapist is saying, but will admit that there are advantages to thinking the way that is being suggested.

If it were not for desirability of thinking, gambling would not exist. There would be no such thing as a state lottery. What causes people to stand in line for hours to purchase a lottery ticket when the jackpot is very high? Most people realize that there is a very low probability of winning the lottery. What causes them to stand in line for hours is the thought, "if only I were to win the lottery, how much better my life would be!" That is desirability of thinking.

So a person might think of herself as unintelligent. Her therapist works at helping her to see that she is much brighter than she has always thought. She does not believe a word of what is told to her, but she will admit that she probably would be happier and pursue more goals if she were to think the way the therapist is suggesting. Realizing the advantages of thinking she is intelligent will help her to look for evidence that supports it—to give it a chance.

Repetition is achieved by simply repeating the new rational thoughts daily as described earlier in this chapter. The more that people repeat thoughts to themselves, or the more a message is repeated to them, the more likely it is that they will come to believe it. I'm sure you have heard people say things like, "he lies so much, after a while he comes to believe his own lies." That's due to repetition.

Evidence is very important in developing long-term thoughts. Many people think thoughts that have a very weak foundation, like a house built on sand. As a result, the thoughts are not durable enough to be helpful in tough times. We want our new, rational thoughts to have a solid foundation.

Sometimes people tell me, "I tried to think that everything would be okay, but I just couldn't keep thinking that way." When I ask them what evidence they had to support this idea that everything would be "okay," they say, "well, none really." This is an example of a thought with a weak foundation. Instead, if a person said, "The reason I'll be okay is because I've gone through this before and survived, and others like me have dealt with similar situations," he or she will be more likely to continue thinking this new thought.

To build a solid foundation for your new, rational thoughts, we are going to look for evidence every day that supports them.

A related issue is **Expert Voice**. The more knowledgeable a person believes the source of information is, the more likely he or she is to take seriously what the source says. Unfortunately, it is the *perception* that the source is knowledgeable that matters, not whether or not the source actually is! While it is a good idea to seek advice from people that have demonstrated that they do have knowledge with something that concerns us, it doesn't hurt to investigate what they tell us to make certain that they are correct. For example, my medical doctor and cardiologist are excellent physicians. I trust them. After all, they saved my life by recognizing that I had advanced cardiovascular disease. Despite that fact, if they prescribe a medication for me, I make certain that the medication does not interact with other medications that I am taking.

Emotional Insight is the result of practice, i.e., repetition, visualization, and physical practice as described earlier in this chapter. Recall that emotional insight is the perception that a thought "feels right." If a thought feels right to a person, he or she is more likely to think and believe it. As was mentioned in this chapter, this "gut thinking" is unfortunate in that just because a thought feels right does not mean it is accurate. Regardless, we want to help make this new, rational thought feel right through practice.

The following is another format that I developed that is based on these four factors that your therapist might use to help you to practice your new thoughts.

Thought to Practice

<u>**Goal:**</u> *To feel calm when seeing my ex-girlfriend and to treat her kindly.*

<u>**Thought:**</u> *Anything that is physically present is "something." Therefore, it is impossible for me to be a "nothing." What I am is a human being. I need no one or nothing for me to be a human being. I was born with the same human worth as everyone else, and no one or nothing can take that away from anyone!*

I didn't need my ex-girlfriend—I only wanted her. Therefore, I'll feel appropriately sad as I think of losing her as a disappointment, not something that is terrible or that I can't stand. Certainly I can stand her breaking up with me, because I am!

The sooner I calmly accept the fact that we ended this relationship, the sooner I will find happiness in another relationship or with something else.

<u>**Desirability**</u>: *When I think this way I'll be much more likely to react calmly when I see my ex-girl-friend.*

<u>**Evidence**</u>:

<u>**Repetition**</u>: *I shall repeat this thought to myself at least five times per day for the next month. I shall practice this thought at the following times:*

<u>**Emotional Insight**</u>: *Practicing my thought will make it "feel right" to me eventually. Therefore, I shall practice it every day.*

The **first step** is to write out your goal statement. This will be the reason to practice the new thought. The **second step** is to write out the new, rational thought to practice. At first, your therapist probably will help you to develop the new thought to make certain that the thought you develop is rational for you. Once you have an adequate understanding of how to develop new thoughts, you will be encouraged to do so on your own and your therapist will provide feedback on them.

The **third step** is to look for evidence every day that supports your new belief. Even if you are uncertain whether or not something is evidence that supports your new belief, write it down. You can discuss what you have written with your therapist.

The **fourth step** is to lay out a schedule to practice (read aloud to yourself) this new belief. Schedule certain times of the day to practice it. The **fifth step** is to make a statement concerning the fact that the new thought will feel comfortable eventually after sufficient practice.

The next chapter discusses another outstanding method of acquiring new thoughts—rational hypnotherapy.

10

Rational Hypnotherapy

A special note about his chapter: Some people are apprehensive about being "hypnotized" because of a fear of losing control of oneself or sometimes due to religious beliefs. Rational Hypnotherapy is a very powerful technique that helps to speed progress in therapy. If you are interested in it but are afraid, your therapist will be happy to discuss your fears. If you have religious objections to it and, therefore, do not want to be hypnotized, you will still do well without it. Rational Hypnotherapy is not a required part of your therapy.

By now, you clearly understand the fact that our thoughts cause our feelings and behaviors. It is also important to know, however, that we acquire our thoughts several different ways. We learn our thoughts by observing how other people think, which is called **Observational Learning.**" If you listen to first-grade children during election years, they will tell you who "should" be president. How do they arrive at their opinions? By listening to their parents, they come to express the same views.

We also learn our thinking through **"Operant Conditioning,"** meaning that we are rewarded or punished in some way for thinking the thoughts we think. When we are rewarded for thinking a certain way, we are more likely to continue thinking that way. When we are punished, we are less likely to think that way again. An example of a thought being punished is a person discovering that his thought, "This machine will give me a can of soda pop," is incorrect when he loses his money to the machine. As a result, he is less likely to think that thought about that machine in the future.

Another way we acquire thoughts is through **"Hypnosis."** Now, you might be thinking to yourself, "Maybe some people acquire thoughts through hypnosis, but I've never been hypnotized. So I must have never acquired thoughts through hypnosis." It is important to understand, though, that we all go through states of hypnosis naturally throughout every day. We go through states of hypnosis as we wake up and as we fall asleep (which happen to be the two best times to learn something). We also go into states of hypnosis when we daydream. Have you ever traveled somewhere, had your mind on something, and the next thing you know you are there and wondered how you arrived at your destination? If so, you've experienced hypnosis. People also go into a state of hypnosis when they experience sudden shock and trauma. If confusion is also experienced during the incident, a person will experience an even deeper state of hypnosis.

One of the best, but most unfortunate examples of this was what most Americans experienced on September 11, 2001. I remember that day vividly. I was at a hotel in Appleton, Wisconsin conducting a seminar for mental health professionals. The seminar began at 8:30 a.m. About ten minutes after the commencement of the seminar, someone entered the room and notified us that an airplane had hit the World Trade Center in New York City. Given our pre-9/11 mentality, we assumed that the plane must have been a small engine plane that had experienced mechanical problems. During the break at 10:00 a.m., we went into the lobby of the hotel and quickly realized that our assumption was way off the mark. The hotel had a very large "Big Screen" television in the lobby, and everyone in the hotel must have been in that lobby. Despite that fact, it was so quiet that I'm sure that we could have heard a pin drop. Everyone was "glued" to the television screen in a rather deep state of hypnosis. What caused the hypnotic state? The traumatic nature of what we witnessed (the death and destruction) along with the confusion we experienced (We couldn't believe what we were witnessing. People do not intentionally fly planes into buildings.) encouraged us to go into that deep state of hypnosis.

When we are in a state of hypnosis, what is said to us, what we think, and messages to which we are exposed are more likely to be taken as a fact, although we might not entirely believe the information. The deeper the state of hypnosis, the less the issue of believability is relevant to whether or not a person acts on that message.

For example, one female client of mine had a problem with social phobia—she was very afraid of being around other people, especially crowds. As a part of her therapy, we elected to do Rational Hypnotherapy. One post-hypnotic suggestion that I gave her (after she was in a good state of hypnosis) was, "Seeing people causes you to relax, and each time that you see people, you do relax twice as quickly as the time before." During the following week's appointment, I asked her how she was doing. She said, "You know, it's the strangest thing. Do you remember last week that you told me that seeing people would cause me to relax? When you told me that, I thought that that was the biggest bunch of nonsense that I had ever heard in my life! But I'll be darned if I'm not relaxed around others!" She had no explanation as to why she was relaxed around people even though she had not *believed* the suggestion when it was presented to her. The reason the suggestion worked was that she was in a good state of hypnosis during the hypnotherapy session and she did not reject the suggestion. In other words, as I gave her the suggestion, had she said to herself, "No, I don't want to be relaxed around people" the suggestion would not have worked.

Therefore, the main reason Rational Living Therapists use hypnotherapy with their clients (with their permission and informed consent) is because *the client does not have to believe the suggestions or messages presented* for those suggestions to become a part of the way the client thinks and behaves. Often psychotherapy or counseling clients *wish* that they believed the positive, rational ideas that their therapists encourage them to believe. They seem to have a hard time doing so at times, though, usually because they see no reason to believe them. With hypnotherapy, the client doesn't have to *believe* those positive messages for the client to begin acting as though he or she believes them!

Another reason Rational Living Therapists use hypnotherapy with their clients is that research has shown that the deeper the state of hypnosis a person is in, the fewer repetitions of the information are needed for the person to learn the information and act on it. Therefore, it is not necessarily the case that a person will be relieved of their problem with one session of hypnotherapy (although I have seen dramatic results often after one hypnotherapy session). However, hypnotherapy will require fewer repetitions of the information for problem resolution to occur than it would with other approaches. As a result, Rational Hypnotherapy is an excellent technique to speed the progress of therapy. Therefore, Rational Hypnotherapy is just another way to help people change the way they think. But the main difference between it and the other approaches described in this book to helping people change their thoughts is that a person doesn't have to believe the new thoughts, and the thoughts are learned more quickly through hypnotherapy. Sometimes Rational Living Therapists suggest that Rational Hypnotherapy be performed early in the therapy process. This is true especially if the client has a problem that makes it difficult for him or her to attend therapy sessions (such as being afraid to leave one's home), or if symptoms are particularly severe. Otherwise, Rational Hypnotherapy is usually conducted toward the end of the Rational Living Therapy process.

Rational Living Therapists usually perform at least two sessions of hypnotherapy—the initial main hypnotherapeutic session and a second session that is recorded on audio tape so that the client can practice self-hypnosis. Self-hypnosis provides the client an excellent way to relax and another great self-counseling technique that can be applied to any problem.

There are many myths and misconceptions concerning hypnosis and hypnotherapy. On the following page is a list of the most common myths, along with their factual counterparts.

Common Myths About
Hypnosis and Hypnotherapy

1. **Myth:** A person is asleep during hypnosis.

   Fact: A person is totally awake during hypnosis.

2. **Myth:** People in a hypnotic state do not know what is going on around them. They totally tune out the surroundings.

   Fact: People in a hypnotic state can hear every sound that they would ordinarily hear. They aware of their surroundings. They are asked to close their eyes, though.

3. **Myth:** The hypnotist can make me do things I don't want to do, like rob a bank or take my clothes off.

   Fact: An ethical Hypnotherapist wouldn't ask a person to do these things to begin with. People can and do reject any suggestion that is contrary to their morals, desires, or survival.

4. **Myth:** A person can get stuck in hypnosis.

   Fact: A person cannot get "stuck" in hypnosis. You go through a semi-hypnotic state every time you wake up and fall asleep. You simply open your eyes.

5. **Myth:** The hypnotist hypnotizes people.

   Fact: Clients hypnotize themselves. The hypnotist just guides them through it.

6. **Myth:** People lose control of themselves when hypnotized.

   Fact: People maintain total control of themselves.

7. **Myth:** I've never been in a hypnotic state.

   Fact: We experience hypnotic states, to some degree, every day.

8. **Myth:** Hypnosis is the work of the Devil. Hypnosis puts you in a vulnerable state that makes it likely that you will be possessed.

   Fact: No evidence of this whatsoever. Many ministers and priests use hypnotherapy.

As you can see, hypnotherapy is a very safe, effective means of helping people rid themselves of old, irrational thoughts and of replacing them with new, rational thoughts. Hypnosis is not sleeping. You do not "go under" like when under general anesthesia for surgery. There is no feeling associated with being in a state of hypnosis. Most people expect to feel some strange, unique feeling that they have never felt before. When they don't, they have the, "I wasn't hypnotized syndrome." However, your therapist (if you chose to do Rational Hypnotherapy) will perform some harmless tests during the hypnotherapy session to make certain that you are in a good state of hypnosis.

Additionally, note that not only do you *not* lose control of yourself during hypnosis, but, in fact, you can be in more control of yourself than you usually are. For example, if someone were to ask you right now to make your right hand completely numb so that a surgeon could operate on it, would you be able to do that? Probably not. But you could make it numb, warm, cold, heavy as a boulder, or a whole host of other sensations while in a state of hypnosis. The possibilities are virtually endless.

There are many ways to perform hypnotherapy. I recommend Rational Hypnotherapy, a technique that I developed that is consistent with the rational philosophy you have been learning in this book. If your therapist does not perform Rational Hypnotherapy, contact the National Association of Cognitive-Behavioral Therapists at 1-800-853-1135 and we will be glad to inform you of our self-hypnosis programs or possibly refer you to a Rational Hypnotherapist in your area.

11

More Rational Techniques

There are eight additional rational self-counseling techniques that I believe are important to include in this book: (1) Breaking Response Chains, (2) Environmental Manipulation, (3) Contingent Reinforcement, (4) Reinforcement of Incompatible Behavior, (5) Putting things into perspective, (6) Time Distancing, (7) "Life is Too Short" Philosophy, and (8) Positive/Negative Imagery. I encourage you to utilize these techniques to make your self-counseling even more successful.

(1) <u>Breaking Response Chains</u>

If we view behavior or reactions as a sequence or chain of events, the earlier in that chain we disrupt it, the more successful we will be in preventing the behavior. Let's take as an example a man (let's call him Paul) who says that he sometimes feels anxious at work, and when he does, he usually stops at a bar on the way home and gets drunk. The **first step** in breaking response chains is to notice a pattern. When do you act or react in the way that you are wanting to change? What tends to remind you to act or react in the undesired way? Knowing the answer to these two questions will help you to know when to implement your new strategy. In this example, Paul gets drunk in reaction to the anxious feelings; therefore, until he learns how to eliminate the thoughts that cause him to feel anxious at work, he will want to use the anxious feelings as a signal that he needs to implement a plan to keep himself from getting drunk.

The **second step** is to plan a course of action that will prevent the undesired behavior or reaction. It is important to develop a plan that will make it nearly impossible to engage in the undesired behavior while implementing it. An excellent strategy for Paul would be to call his wife when he feels anxious and ask her to pick him up or follow him home after work.

The **third step** is to begin acting on the plan. Make a sincere statement to yourself that you refuse to act or react in the old, undesired way, and instead will put the plan into action. When Paul feels anxious at work, he tells himself, "I refuse to drink on the way home, and, instead, I'll call my wife and have her follow me home."

There are many situations in which breaking response chains can be very helpful. If, for example, you know that discussions of certain unimportant topics tend to lead to arguments, find a way to change the subject early in the discussion. Think about how breaking response chains could benefit you.

(2) <u>Environmental Manipulation</u>

Environmental manipulation is creating an environment for yourself that will make it more likely that you will succeed. Environmental manipulation is particularly helpful for, but not limited to, "habit control." For example, when working with people who are wanting to lose weight, I encourage them to seek an appropriate diet plan that their physician has approved. Once they understand the diet plan and what they are to eat, I encourage them to remove any food items from their home that are not on the plan (unless there are others in the home that intend to eat them). The reason for removing these items from their home is not because they have no ability to refuse to eat them (of course they do), but because there is no rational reason to place oneself in a position to be tempted.

When people seek to quit smoking gradually, by weekly reducing the amount they smoke, I encourage them to keep in their home only as many cigarettes as they intend to smoke for the day. Obviously, people have the ability to purchase more; but if it takes some effort to travel to a store to purchase them, they have time to talk themselves out of smoking more cigarettes than they had intended.

Alcoholics Anonymous encourages people who have had a habit of drinking irrationally to avoid places where alcohol is served, particularly bars and nightclubs. I often encourage people to surround themselves with people who have achieved what they want to achieve, who are rationally positive and optimistic, and avoid those who are irrationally pessimistic. Remember, though, that we maintain total control over our thoughts, feelings, and behaviors. So we need not concern ourselves that we necessarily will think pessimistically if we are around others who do so. We do stand a greater chance of *talking ourselves* into thinking pessimistically, though, if the people around us do so.

(3) Contingent Reinforcement

A reinforcer is anything that increases the likelihood that a behavior will be repeated. Reinforcement is using a reinforcer to encourage a behavior, like a reward for doing well. Contingent reinforcement means that for someone to receive the reward, they must do something to earn it. Contingent reinforcement is often used in child rearing with much success. Adults, though, are on contingent reinforcement schedules as well. An employer is unlikely to pay an employee if he or she does not work. Spouses are less likely to do kind things for each other if there isn't some amount of reciprocity.

Sometimes contingent reinforcement is intentionally self-imposed. For example, a person working at motivating herself to read her homework assignment might make watching her favorite television show contingent upon reading it—if she does not read the assignment, she will deny herself of watching the program. This approach certainly does require some self-discipline. However, self-discipline only means that a person has clearly defined goals that are very important, that he or she is keeping mindful of those goals, and that he or she realizes that a strategy like contingent reinforcement is an important part of achieving those goals.

(4) Reinforcement of Incompatible Behavior

An important fact about the human brain is that it does not like a vacuum, meaning that if we eliminate a behavior, but do not replace it with a different behavior, we tend to revert to the old behavior. So developing a replacement behavior is very important. As long as we are going to develop a replacement behavior—a new way to act and react, why not make that replacement behavior incompatible with the original? An incompatible replacement behavior is one that would make engaging in the original behavior difficult.

You might have seen the public service announcements that make statements, like, "it's hard to smoke marijuana while playing a tuba." These announcements are encouraging replacement behaviors to using drugs that are incompatible with using them. If you are wanting to eliminate a habit, develop replacement behaviors that are incompatible with that habit. If you tend to bite your fingernails while watching television, place your hands in your pockets whenever you watch your favorite shows, at least until the habit is broken. If you tend to smoke while driving, make a concerted effort to keep both hands on the steering wheel while driving. If you tend to drink alcohol excessively in the evenings, find an activity, like a martial arts class to fill the time.

(5) Putting Things into Perspective

Whether we intend to or not, we make comparisons on a daily basis. We rate people, for example, in terms of attractiveness, cooperativeness, intelligence, willingness to listen, etc…

When we say, "That person is not very intelligent," we are rating that person by some standard of intelligence. This is why we do not think of everyone as equally intelligent. In psychology, we call this a **figure-ground comparison**. For example, a person might say, "President Clinton is a terrific president compared to President Carter, but a lousy president compared to President Reagan." The perception of the situation depends on to what it is being compared. It is important for us to rate our problems as well, rather than treating every personally negative situation as being equally bad, and, therefore, having the same negative emotional reaction to all problems.

For example, one day I was traveling to my office with a long day ahead of me. I knew that I was going to have a very busy schedule that day. What made matters much worse for me was the fact that I had a very bad headache. I was stopped at a traffic light when I happened to notice a man getting out of a car at a grocery store. He seemed to struggle to get out of the car, and when he was out of it, I realized why—he was disabled. He needed braces to walk, which he used with a lot of effort to get into the store. Seeing this man's situation made me realize that my headache and schedule for the day really were not so bad. I'm sure the man would have loved to have traded places with me.

Sometimes people get the impression, though, that they do not have a right to be upset about their situations because others have it worse than they do. Putting things into perspective has nothing to do with denying yourself the right to be upset. You always have the option of exercising your biological right to making yourself as upset as you want to be. However, putting things into perspective helps you to be only as upset as you want to be.

(6) <u>Time Distancing</u>

If you upset yourself about something, ask yourself, "Is it likely that I'll be as upset about this situation tomorrow, or next week, or next month, or next year as I am right now?" If your answer to this question is "no," then it does not make any rational sense to be as upset about it now. However, if you believe that you will be just as upset next week as you currently are, that is not proof that your thinking makes rational sense. The only reason you would continue to upset yourself next week would be that you would continue to believe the same upsetting beliefs that you currently believe. Ask yourself, "Why would I not be as upset about it tomorrow as I am now?" The usual answers include:

–I will not be as tired tomorrow as I am today;

–I probably will not have the headache tomorrow that I have today;

–This has nothing to do with what is happening tomorrow or any other day;

–I'll probably have come up with a solution by then;

–I will not have as much going on tomorrow, so that will give me a chance to work on this better;

–I know that I'm only thinking this way because I'm already upset about something else that happened today; or

–I'll be used to it by then.

Remember that "time" does not heal wounds. Time only gives us the opportunity to talk ourselves out of feeling miserable. So if a person would not feel as upset a week later as she currently feels, that only means that she would have found some way to talk herself out of it. If she can do it now, she will save herself a week's worth of misery!

(7) <u>"Life is Too Short" Philosophy</u>

Existential psychologists and philosophers say that life means nothing without death. If there were no ending to life, living would not be worth much because there would be an endless supply of days.

Of course, everyone must die at some point. Acknowledging and accepting that fact helps us to appreciate the life we do have. Therefore, should you make yourself consistently upset about anything, ask yourself, "Is this how I want to spend my days, feeling this miserable?" or "If I knew that I would die tomorrow, would I be as upset about this as I am now, or would it seem trivial?"

(8) <u>Positive/Negative Imagery</u>

Positive/Negative Imagery is another technique that is helpful to eliminate problem behavior and replace them with rational actions.

Positive imagery encourages positive, rational behavior. It is visualizing a positive outcome that results from rational behavior. Negative imagery is the opposite—it discourages irrational behavior through visualizing a very negative outcome that results from irrational behavior. I recommend that you first practice the negative imagery then immediately move to the positive imagery. For example, I mentioned earlier that I had coronary bypass surgery. My doctors tell me that my arteries were blocked because of very high cholesterol, and that it was important for me to adhere to a very strict low fat, low cholesterol diet. However, I loved the foods that partially caused my cholesterol to be so high—cheese, red meat, hamburgers, and the like.

To develop a distaste for these foods, and a liking for heart-friendly food, I performed practice sessions during which I first imagined myself eating a hamburger and immediately dropping dead from a heart attack! I also imagined myself eating cheese and red meat, and immediately pictured myself lying in a hospital bed as I had following my surgery. After I upset myself with those images, I then calmed myself through progressive relaxation and imagined myself as a healthy, vibrant eighty-year-old eating pasta and vegetables and enjoying them! After a while, the artery-clogging foods certainly lost their appeal, while the heart-friendly foods became very appealing.

12

Conclusion

Well, there you have it—my guide to living a healthy, happy life, no matter what! With practice and at least occasional reminders, there is every reason to believe that you can utilize these rational self-counseling skills for the rest of your life.

I hope that you found this book informative and inspiring. I would love to hear from you about your experience with it. Please feel free to contact me at:

National Association of Cognitive-Behavioral Therapists
Attention: Aldo R. Pucci
P.O. Box 2195
Weirton, WV 26062.

You may also e-mail me at aldo@nacbt.org. Also, please feel free to visit the NACBT website at: http://www.nacbt.org

Additionally, if you would like to be on our mailing list to be informed of products, services, and workshops we offer, simply contact us by any of the means listed above. For therapists wishing to learn more about Rational Living Therapy, feel free to visit our web site at http://www.rational-living-therapy.org

It's been my pleasure to share with you the philosophy and techniques that I have described in this book. I certainly wish you well.

Rationally yours,
Aldo Pucci

End-Of-Therapy Assessment

Please complete the following questionnaire honestly. This will help you and your therapist assess what you are experiencing, how you are thinking, and how you are feeling.

Circle the answer that best represents your situation.

	Strongly Disagree	Disagree	Neutral	Agree	Strongly Agree
1. Things in my life are different than they should be.	1	2	3	4	5
2. People make me upset.	1	2	3	4	5
3. I can't stand certain things in my life.	1	2	3	4	5
4. I need to think well of myself before I can do certain things.	1	2	3	4	5
5. There are things in my life that are simply awful and terrible.	1	2	3	4	5
6. How I feel depends on how people treat me.	1	2	3	4	5
7. Certain situations make me upset.	1	2	3	4	5
8. People can't feel and act better until their situation changes.	1	2	3	4	5
9. You can't trust someone again after they have violated your trust.	1	2	3	4	5
10. People need to be concerned about other peoples' opinions.	1	2	3	4	5
11. I have a right to be upset.	1	2	3	4	5
12. There isn't much hope for me to feel or act differently because I have tried before and failed. That means I can't.	1	2	3	4	5
13. It's important for me to focus on how I feel and what I do as the main indicators of how well I am doing in therapy.	1	2	3	4	5

End-Of-Therapy Assessment

Please complete the following questionnaire honestly. This will help you and your therapist assess what you are experiencing, how you are thinking, and how you are feeling.

Circle the answer that best represents your situation.

	Strongly Disagree	Disagree	Neutral	Agree	Strongly Agree
14. If I don't see it, it doesn't exist.	1	2	3	4	5
15. I just can't cope with things.	1	2	3	4	5
16. I need medication to make me feel better.	1	2	3	4	5
17. I believe that if I just get things off of my chest, I will feel much better.	1	2	3	4	5
18. If I do something good, I should be rewarded.	1	2	3	4	5
19. If I treat people well, they should treat me well, too.	1	2	3	4	5
20. If I am the only one thinking a certain way, then I must be wrong.	1	2	3	4	5
21. If it feels wrong, it must be wrong.	1	2	3	4	5
22. If it feels right, it must be right.	1	2	3	4	5
23. It's important for a person to follow his or her gut instinct.	1	2	3	4	5
24. If I do something wrong, I should punish myself for it.	1	2	3	4	5

Appendix

Camera Checks

The following is a list of common expressions used in our society that would not pass the camera check of perceptions as they are typically used. If you think of other expressions that you would like to share, please send them to: NACBT, P.O. Box 2195, Weirton, WV 26062 or e-mail them to me at: camera-checks@nacbt.org.

1. Fell all to pieces
2. Dirty rat
3. Blew up
4. End of my rope
5. Trapped
6. End-of-the-world
7. Scared to death
8. Nervous breakdown
9. Lost my mind
10. Crapped on me
11. Blimp, Whale
12. Jerk
13. S.O.B.
14. "A" Hole
15. Tore me apart
16. Apart at the seams
17. Broken heart
18. Jerk my chain
19. Floored me
20. Pain in the Butt
21. Stole my heart

22. Moron
23. Idiot
24. Dummy
25. It's killing me
26. Beast
27. Ugly as Sin
28. I died
29. Splitting Headache
30. Doesn't have the guts
31. Jumped down my throat
32. Get off of my back
33. Loser
34. Worked myself to death
35. Gutless mouse
36. He Rode Me
37. Eating Me Up
38. Cold Hearted
39. Went off the deep End
40. Cracked Up
41. Went Nuts

References

Babyak, Michael, Blumenthal, James A., Herman, Steve, Khatri, Parinda, Doraiswamy, Murali, Moore, Kathleen, Craighead, W. Edward, Baldewicz, Teri T., and Krishnan, K. Ranga. (2000). Exercise treatment for major depression: maintenance of therapeutic benefit at 10 months. *Psychosomatic Medicine, 62(5)*, 633-38.

Beck, A.T. (1976). *Cognitive Therapy and the Emotional Disorders.* New York, NY: International Universities Press.

Benkert, O. (1976). Effect of parachlorophenylalanine and 5-hydroxytryptophan on human sexual behavior. *Monographs in Neural Sciences*, 3, 88-93.

Benkert, O. (1975). Studies on pituitary hormones and releasing hormones in depression and sexual impotence. *Progress in Brain Research*, 42, 25-36.

Blumenthal, James A., Babyak, Michael A., Moore, Kathleen A., Craighead, W. Edward, Herman, Steve, Khatri, Parinda, Waugh, Robert, Napolitano, Melissa A., Forman, Leslie M., Appelbaum, Mark, Doraiswamy P., Murali, and Krishnan, K., Ranga. (1999). Effects of exercise training on older patients with major depression. *Archives of Internal Medicine*, 159, 2349-2356.

Bloomfield, H. (1998). *Healing Anxiety Naturally.* New York, NY: HarperCollins.

Brenner, R., Azbel, V., Madhusoodanan, S., Pawlowska, M. (2000). Comparison of an extract of hypericum and sertraline in the treatment of depression: a double blind, randomized pilot study. *Clinical Therapy*, 22(4), 411-19.

Burns, David (1980). *Feeling Good: The New Mood Therapy.* New York, NY: Signet.

Crook, William G. (1987). *Solving the Puzzle of Your Hard-To-Raise Child.* New York: Random House.

Ellis, Albert (1988). *How to Stubbornly Refuse to Make Yourself Miserable About Anything—Yes, Anything.* New York: Carol Publishing Group.

Ellis, Albert (2002). *Overcoming Resistance: A Rational Emotive Behavior Therapy Integrated Approach.* New York, NY: Springer Publishing Company.

Holmes, T.H., & Rahe, R.H. (1967). The social readjustment rating scale. *Journal of Psychosomatic Research*, 11, 213-218.

Holmes, T.H., & Ruch, L.O. (1971). Scaling of life change: comparison of direct and indirect methods. *Journal of Psychosomatic Research*, 15, 221-227. Korf, J, van den Burg, W., and Van den Hoofdakker, RH. (1983). Acid metabolites and precursor amino acids of 5-hydroxytryptamine and dopamine in affective and other psychiatric disorders. *Psychiatr Clin* (Basel), 16(1), 1-16.

Maslow, A. (1954). Motivation and personality. New York: Harper.

Maultsby, M.C. (1975). *Help Yourself to Happiness.* New York: Institute for Rational Emotive Therapy.

Maultsby, M.C. (1984). *Rational Behavior Therapy.* Appleton, WI: Rational Self-Help Aids/I'ACT.

Peet, M. & Horrobin, D. (2002). A dose-ranging study of the effects of ethyl-eicosapentaenoate in patients with ongoing depression despite apparently adequate treatment with standard drugs. *Archives of General Psychiatry,* 59, 913-919.

Poldinger, W., Calanchini, B., and Schwarz, W. (1991). A functional-dimensional approach to depression: serotonin deficiency as a target syndrome in a comparison of 5-hydroxy-tryptophan and fluvoxamine. *Psychopathology,* 24, 53-81.

Ross, Julia (2002). *The Mood Cure.* New York, NY: Penguin Putnam, Inc.

Schmidt, Michael A. (1997). *Smart Fats: How Dietary Fats and Oils Affect Mental, Physical and Emotional Intelligence.* Berkley, CA: Frog Ltd.

Schrader, E. (2000). Equivalence of St. John's wort extract and fluoxetine: a randomized, controlled study in mild-moderate depression. *International Journal of Clinical Psychopharmacology,* 15(2), 61-8.

Werbach, M. (1991). *Nutritional Influences on Mental Illness.* Tarzana, CA: Third Line Press.

Whitaker, Julian (1995). *Dr. Whitaker's Guide to Natural Healing.* Rocklin, CA: Prima Publishing.

Yerkes R., & Dodson, J. (1908). The relation of strength of stimulus to rapidity of habit-formation. *Journal of Comparative Neurology and Psychology,* 18, 459-482.

About the Author

Aldo R. Pucci, MA, DCBT is the president of the National Association of Cognitive-Behavioral Therapists, an association that he formed in 1995. Pucci was trained originally in cognitive-behavioral therapy by one of its pioneers, Dr. Maxie C. Maultsby, Jr. Dr. Maultsby, who recently retired from Howard University as the chairperson of the Department of Psychiatry, is the originator of Rational Behavior Therapy. Pucci modified Dr. Maultsby's approach to include original techniques and philosophies (like the replacement of "self-esteem" with the "Four A's") and hypnotherapy. The result is what Pucci calls "Rational Living Therapy." Pucci is the president of the Rational Living Therapy Institute. Pucci has served as an adjunct faculty member in the Graduate Counseling Program at Franciscan University of Steubenville. He has taught cognitive-behavioral therapy and Rational Living Therapy to thousands of mental health professionals throughout the United States. His seminars and workshops receive rave reviews.

Pucci has extensive experience with the application of cognitive-behavioral therapy both in community mental health centers and in private practice. He has helped people with a wide range of problems and concerns help themselves through rational self-counseling. The NACBT's Board of Advisors awarded Pucci the Diplomate in Cognitive-Behavioral Therapy. He also is a Licensed Professional Counselor, a Certified Clinical Hypnotherapist, and a Certified Medical Hypnotherapist. Pucci lives in Weirton, West Virginia (a suburb of Pittsburgh, PA) with his wife, Sandy, and their two children, Aldo Jr. and Maria.

978-0-595-38076-3
0-595-38076-X